Mat. 6 = 5
Don't B tra
speak fai-

5

MW01531130

GLORIFYING GOD THROUGH STEWARDSHIP

THE PURPOSE OF LIVING

NATE HOLCOMB

Him Publishing

The Purpose of Living
By Nate Holcomb

Copyright © 2014
Nate Holcomb

Printed in the United States of America

ISBN: 978-1-930918-37-5

Him Publishing
P.O. Box 960
Copperas Cove, TX 76522
www.HimPublishing.com

Him Publishing, Inc. is a ministry of
The Cathedral of Central Texas,
CHRISTIAN HOUSE OF PRAYER MINISTRIES, INC.
www.chop.org

For ye are bought with a price:
therefore glorify God in your body, and
in your spirit, which are God's.
(1 Corinthians 6:20)

CONTENTS

INTRODUCTION 7

{ S E C T I O N   I } 11

JESUS: HAVE THE PREEMINENCE 13

GLORIFYING GOD THROUGH STEWARDSHIP 25

SPENDING AND INVESTING IN LIVING.........................39

{ S E C T I O N   I I } 53

THE PRINCIPLE OF GIVING 55

HOW YOU VIEW GOD..71

LIVING IN GOD'S ECONOMY — PT. 1 85

LIVING IN GOD'S ECONOMY — PT. 2 95

{ S E C T I O N   I I I } 109

THE PATTERN OF RECEIVING......................................111

FORGIVENESS KEEPS THE HEART BELIEVING 123

HARVEST GUARANTEED 135

HOW TO AVOID A BAD HARVEST................................. 147

INTRODUCTION

AT SOME POINT IN LIFE every person aspires to find their calling; for once it is discovered, fulfillment and satisfaction ensues. But on a wider scale, to find The Purpose of Living transcends personal vocation and ventures into the impact on the very essence of life itself.

To find The Purpose of Living elevates the stature and station of a person's life because he or she lays hold of a key which, once turned, unlocks principles conducive to nothing but provision, promotion, and prosperity in every aspect of life.

There is a way to rise above the squalid living of low expectations, and soar to altitudes yielding favorable expectations. And you can start right where you are, beginning with five blessings heaven has already bestowed upon you: your time, talents, gifts, possessions, and money.

Perhaps you have never viewed these endowments as anything spectacular; but once fitted into the lock of glorifying God, they release the bounty of heaven.

In this book Nate Holcomb teaches that glorifying God with your time, talents, gifts, possessions, and money is a form of economics. God has sown these things in you; and in serving Him with them, you're giving Him a return with interest on His investment.

Learn how to tap into the spiritual law of "give and it shall be given to you again," by discovering the strategy of giving what you need to receive, giving what you want to receive, and its reciprocal effects on your life.

Insights from this book can help you unlock the deadbolt of lack and insufficiency, while opening doors to the purpose of living, which includes the principle of giving, and the pattern of receiving.

THE PURPOSE OF LIVING

{SECTION I}

1

JESUS: HAVE THE PREEMINENCE

And he is the head of the body, the church: who is the beginning, the firstborn from the dead; that in all things he might have the preeminence. (Colossians 1:18)

VINE'S EXPOSITORY DICTIONARY of Old Testament and New Testament Words translate preeminence as *protos*. This Greek word *protos* means, *"to be first."* To be preeminent (*protos*), is used specifically of Christ in relation to His church.

We find Paul encouraging the church of Colossae that in all things Jesus is to be first. Interestingly, Paul used the word *might* in conjunction with Jesus having the preeminence. For Jesus to have preeminence; we must yield the first place to Him. Paul in essence was asking the church, "Are we going to give Jesus the place that He deserves?"

WE MUST KEEP JESUS FIRST

Giving Jesus the preeminence, calls for us to be committed to Him. It is prayer that connects us to God. The following passage is the prayer Paul taught the church of Colossae for the purpose of making that commitment.

For this cause we also, since the day we heard it, do not cease to pray for you, and to desire that ye might be filled with the knowledge of his will in all wisdom and spiritual understanding; That ye might walk worthy of the Lord unto all pleasing, being fruitful in every good work, and increasing in the knowledge of God; Strengthened with all might, according to his glorious power, unto all patience and longsuffering with joyfulness; Giving thanks unto the Father, which hath made us meet to be partakers of the inheritance of the saints in light: Who hath delivered us from the power of darkness, and hath translated us into the kingdom of his dear Son: In whom we have redemption through his blood, even the forgiveness of sins: Who is the image of the invisible God, the firstborn of every creature. For by him were all things created, that are in heaven, and that are in earth, visible and invisible, whether they be thrones, or dominions, or principalities, or powers: all things were created by him, and for him: And he is before all things, and by him all things consist. And he is the head of the body, the church: who is the beginning, the firstborn from the dead; that in all things he might have the preeminence. (Colossians 1:9-18)

Many times people say, *"God has a place in my life."* However, the Lord Jesus is not looking for *a place* in our lives. He does not want *"a place,"* He has to have *"the place"* He made *for Himself*—**The Preeminence!**

God gave the Ten Commandments to Moses. The first commandment is, *"Thou shalt have no other gods before me (Ex. 20:3)."* Because God created a place in our hearts especially for Himself; we will never be satisfied unless He is glorified by having 1st place. Without the Lord, our lives are void of His victory. No matter how many people are around, if Jesus is not first, life can be full of sadness without the possibility of gladness.

> *Or who hath first given to him, and it shall be*
> *recompensed unto him again? For of him, and*
> *through him, and to him, are all things: to whom*
> *be glory forever. Amen. (Romans 11:35-36)*

> *And he is before all things, and by him all things consist.*
> *And he is the head of the body, the church: who is the*
> *beginning, the firstborn from the dead; that in all things*
> *he might have the preeminence. (Colossians 1:17-18)*

The prefix **pre** means before everything and anything. **Eminence** is related to a king or in our case Jesus. Jesus is Lord and because He has the preeminence, He has Lordship. He is *the head of the body*, and a body without *a head is dead*. Conversely, two heads on one body is unnatural. Jesus is the head; therefore, He must have the preeminence.

Some don't seek Jesus to make Him *first*; instead they seek Him for fire insurance. They simply do not want to go to hell. Although there are Christians catching all kinds of hell in the earth, Jesus says, the gates of hell shall not prevail against the church (Matt. 16:18).

Jesus declared to the seven churches of Asia, *"I know your works... (Rev. 2:2),"* but to the church of Ephesus, He stated, His grievance of how they left their first love (Rev. 2:4). Some of us have never made Jesus our first love and because of this, we lack victory and *good* success. All success is not good. The problem with *good* is it has one too many o's. Everything good is not God, however, everything God is good (Jos. 1:8).

O death, where is thy sting? O grave, where is thy
victory? But thanks be to God, which giveth us the victory
through our Lord Jesus Christ. (1 Corinthians 15:55, 57)

WE MUST MAKE JESUS LORD

No place in the Bible suggests Jesus as Savior apart from
being Lord. Many have opened the door allowing Jesus to
be Savior but some have closed the door to His Lordship.
The Bible teaches the principles of Jesus' Lordship which
denote: *Jesus must be Lord of all, in all, through all, or not
at all.*

There is no halfway house with God. We cannot invite God
into our house and confine Him to one room. He has seniority
and He wants authority over the entire house. Jesus taught:
"Thy kingdom come. Thy will be done in earth, as it is in heaven
(Matt. 6:10)." His will is to be done on earth and in our hearts. It
begins in our heart and moves into our house.

God the Father has made Jesus Lord! The Scripture records:
*"...God hath made that same Jesus, whom ye have crucified, both
Lord and Christ (Acts 2:36)."* He's already Lord! However, the
question remains, *"Is Jesus your Lord?"* Jesus noted: *"And why
call ye me, Lord, Lord, and do not the things which I say* (Lu.
6:46)?" Therefore, every child of God must make Jesus Lord.

King David the sweet psalmist of Israel said, *"The Lord
is my shepherd, I shall not want (Ps. 23:1)."* Jesus is the **Good
Shepherd**, **Great Shepherd**, and **Chief Shepherd** (John 10:11,
Heb. 13:20, 1 Pet. 5:4). Isaiah said: *"All we* (not all ye) *like sheep
have gone astray (Isa. 53:6 parenthesis added)."* We must make it
personal: Jesus Christ the Lord is our Shepherd.

David was in the valley and remarked: *"He maketh me to lie
down in green pastures: he leadeth me beside the still waters (Ps.*

23:2)." Sheep are afraid of everything and anything. Running water scares sheep, so God causes us to lie down beside still water. With His rod and staff He comforts us, He prepares a table before us in the presence of our enemies: He anoints our heads with oil; our cups run over (vv. 4-5). David concluded: *"Surely goodness and mercy shall follow me all the days of my life... (Ps. 23:6)."* David is in the valley; however, because he made Jesus his Lord, he was given rest in the midst of trouble.

If the Lord is not our shepherd in the valley, the devil will ultimately break and tear us down. Jesus Christ is the One that lifts us, and sets our feet upon a rock, and establishes our goings (Ps. 40:2). If Jesus is the Lord of our life, He has the preeminence. Every day we wake up we must declare, *"This is the day which the Lord hath made (Ps. 118:24)!"*

Jesus is Lord! When we give Jesus His office place, He will do His office work. He will persistently show that the battle is not ours, but God's (2 Chr. 20:15). If we just hold our peace and let the Lord fight the battle, victory shall be ours. Some of us only know Jesus as Savior not as Lord. When we crown Him Lord, it doesn't matter what we are going through, our house will not fall.

THE LORD WILL WORK IT OUT

James, the brother of Jesus, says: *"Ye have heard of the patience of Job, and have seen the end of the Lord (Jam. 5:11)."* In other words James was declaring, allow Jesus to work it out. When we allow Jesus to be Lord, there is an end to our suffering. Job emphatically declared: *"If a man die, shall he live again? All the days of my appointed time will I wait, till my change come (Job 14:14)."*

The last independent decision we made should have been

to make Jesus the Lord of our life. After that, we must allow Him to govern our affairs. People who fail to make Jesus Lord experience *stress, struggle*, and *strain*. On the other hand, people who yield to His Lordship receive *enjoyment, excitement*, and *fulfillment* even when hell breaks loose.

Joseph was thrown into a pit by his brothers. From the pit, he went to Potiphar's house and eventually to prison. From prison Joseph landed in the palace (Gen. 41:1-57). Once in the palace, Pharaoh entrusted Joseph with everything concerning the nation; and only Pharaoh ruled above him (Gen. 41:40-45). Later, Joseph's brothers feared that he would kill them, but he said: *"Am I in the place of God (Gen. 50:19)?"* Joseph further explained, what his brothers meant for evil, God made it work together for good (v 20). Joseph gave God first place in His life, and God worked everything out for him.

I have learned; **never try to figure out what only God can work out.** Many people have a way of putting themselves in the place of God, therefore having to work or figure things out for themselves. We are not in the place of God. If Jesus is our head He is preeminent.

Elijah followed God's instructions (1 Ki. 18:42-44). He put his head between his knees and started praying. Then he told his servant *"Go up!"* The servant went up and returned back saying, *"Nothing is happening."* Elijah told his servant to go up again, because he was hearing a sound. The servant came back saying, *"I do not see anything!"* Elijah told him to go up again not on the basis of what's seen, but on what's heard. Something is happening even when it looks like nothing is happening. **When we are down to nothing; God is up to something!**

When we give God control, He gives his beloved sleep (Ps. 127:2). He *"neither sleeps nor slumbers (Ps. 121:4)."* Since the Lord is awake, we can sleep. God is working it out. Even when it looks like nothing is happening just go head and *praise the Lord.*

THE LORD WILL MAKE A WAY

O the depth of the riches both of the wisdom and knowledge of God! how unsearchable are his judgments, and his ways past finding out! (Romans 11:33)

The word judgments in the text denote God's decisions. His ways are past our understanding. God told Moses to bring the children of Israel out of Egypt. Moses and Israel had the Egyptians behind them and the Red Sea before them. Israel had no way out. At this point, God commanded: *"Stand still and see the salvation of the Lord."* The salvation of the Lord is the way of the Lord.

We may say, *"There's no way!"* However, with God all things are possible. How did God open the Red Sea and sustain it? Did Moses have to measure the Red Sea? No. All he had to do was obey God and stretch out the rod. Even though Moses was shaking on the rock, the Rock was not shaking under him.

For who hath known the mind of the Lord? Or who has been his counselor? (Romans 11:34)

Sometimes we can be guilty of trying to counsel the Lord. This happens when we tell God we are going to do this or that; go here or there.

In Romans 11, the scripture asks, *"Who has known the mind of the Lord"* (v. 34). Paul then says, *"For who hath known the **mind of the Lord**, that he may instruct him? But we have **the mind of Christ"** (1 Cor. 2:16).* To the church at Philippi Paul also says,

"Let this mind be in you, which was also in Christ Jesus..." (Phil. 2:5).

Here's the revelation of a difference: we have *the **mind of Christ*** but we do not have *the **mind of the Lord*** (1 Cor. 2:16). Having the mind of Christ means we can learn how to respond to life's difficulties. However, only the Lord has ultimate control and wisdom concerning our direction in life. Therefore, let Jesus have His place.

Jesus has His place as Lord, and as the Lord, He makes a way where there is no way. Proverbs 3:5-6 tells us to, *"Trust in the Lord with all thine heart; and lean not unto thy own understanding. In all thy ways acknowledge him, and he shall direct thy paths."*

The previous scripture conveys:
1. *God **chooses** the way*
2. *God **confirms** the way*
3. *God **clears** the way*

Jesus does it all when He has preeminence. The word "confirm" means He gives us a peace that *"passes all of our understanding (Phil. 4:7)."* In the midst of trials there is a peace on the inside of us because He is Lord. He will work it out for us if we trust His way with all our heart and lean not to our own understanding.

We acknowledge Him in all our ways because we don't know it all. Nevertheless, we do not have to know it all because *we know the One that knows it all!* We must come to a place of complete comfort with Jesus being our Lord, by acknowledging, *"Lord, I don't know the way."*

Jehoshaphat and the children of Judah were surrounded by three invading armies. Their enemies where coming from every direction. Jehoshaphat said unto the Lord, *"I don't know what else to do, but my eyes are upon thee."* Afterwards, the Lord spoke and told Jehoshaphat he didn't need to fight in the battle, he just needed to get excited and watch God work His way (2 Chron. 20:12-17).

The Lord told Jehoshaphat and the people to follow His lead. Like Jehoshaphat, we need to follow Jesus' lead. Jehoshaphat asked the LORD God what he was to do. The LORD said, *"Send Judah first!"* The LORD did not command them to throw spears and knives; instead He told him to send Judah first. Judah is the tribe that is filled with praise. Judah's responsibility was to praise the LORD. As ordered, Judah started praising, magnifying, and glorifying God. And when they arrived at the battle, it was over. All they had to do was pick up the spoils because the enemy was already destroyed (2 Chron. 20:25). If we hold our peace and let the Lord fight our battle victory shall be ours (Exo. 14:14). He told us in all our ways to acknowledge Him and He will direct our paths (Prov. 3:6).

Wisdom is the principle thing; therefore get wisdom: and with all thy getting, get understanding. (Proverbs 4:7)

Trust in the Lord with all thine heart; and lean not unto thine own understanding. (Proverbs 3:5)

God wants us to have His understanding. The word *understand* is a compound word comprised of the words **under** and **stand**. The word *under* means *to yield; submit* or simply *get under*. What are we to get under? We must get under Jesus' Lordship. He is the head; we are a part of the body. The body goes under the head and not the other way around. We must get in our place and not try to get into God's place. We get His understanding by yielding and submitting to His will.

The word *stand* means *a point of view* and *a position that we take*. Once Jesus is Lord, we have no point of view. This is why He says with all thy getting, *get the Lord's understanding* because we have none. What is His point of view? What is His position? If we know His position then we know our position. *"For in him we live, and move, and have our being..."* (Acts 17:28). We do not have to lean to our own understanding. God already has the plan for our lives. This is why the Lord is called, *"The Man with the Plan."*

The LORD told Joshua He would give Israel the Promised Land. The very first battle for Joshua and the Israelites was a fortified city called Jericho. None could go in and none could go out (Jos. 6:1-27). While Joshua was trying to figure the way, there stood a Man with His sword drawn. When Joshua saw him he asked, *"Are you come for us or for them?"* The Man said: *"Nay; but as captain of the host of the LORD am I now come"* (Jos. 5:14).

Many scholars believe the *"Captain of the Host"* is a theophany (a pre-incarnate manifestation of Jesus Christ). As Captain of the host of the Lord, Jesus conveys: ***I do not come to take sides; I come to take over!*** All we have to do is follow God's plan and allow Him to have His way.

> *Consider what I say; and the Lord give thee*
> *understanding in all things. (2 Timothy 2:7)*

As we consider all that has been written in this chapter and meditate on it, the Lord will give us His understanding and work everything out His way.

CHAPTER ONE
QUESTIONS FOR REFLECTIONS

How are you to keep Jesus first in your life?

....

....

....

....

....

....

If Jesus is not Lord of your life, how will you make Him Lord?

....

....

....

....

....

....

The Bible describes Jesus as a shepherd. What are the
three kinds of shepherds discussed in this chapter?

1. ....

2. ....

3. ....

What should be the last independent decision you make in life?

....

....

....

....

....

....

What is the difference between having the mind
of Christ and the mind of the Lord?

....

....

....

....

....

....

Proverbs 3:5-6 reveals three distinct ways of God, what are they?

....

....

....

....

....

....

What does it mean to get the Lord's understanding about your life?

....

....

....

....

....

....

2

GLORIFYING GOD
THROUGH STEWARDSHIP

Then drew near unto him all the publicans and sinners for to hear him. And the Pharisees and scribes murmured, saying, This man receiveth sinners, and eateth with them. (Luke 15:1-2)

ALTHOUGH THE PHARISEES should have led the lost to the Lord; and been established as good examples of stewards for the souls of men, they did not. However, Jesus Christ died for and received sinners—thus making Him the greatest steward ever.

As a great steward, the Lord Jesus Christ did not teach many different things; however, He taught a few things many different ways. In the gospel according to St. Luke chapter 15, Jesus taught a parable about "The Prodigal Son." I consider this the "Crowning Jewel" of all His teachings.

LOST AND FOUND

A shepherd lost his **sheep**. The shepherd left the flock of ninety-nine and went after the one lost in the wilderness. Upon finding the sheep, he hoisted him upon his shoulders and returned home. Once home, the elated shepherd called his neighbors and friends to rejoice with him. Celebration was in order because the precious and valuable was lost and found (Lu. 15:3-6).

A woman lost her **silver**. She had ten pieces of silver and lost one. Even though only one piece was missing, it was part of a set, and without the missing piece of silver, the value of the set was diminished. Seeking feverishly to find the missing piece, she swept through the house until it was found. She called her neighbors and friends to rejoice with her. They rejoiced because the precious and valuable was lost and found (Lu. 15:8-9).

A father lost his youngest **son**. The son went out and wasted his inheritance. Afterwards, he realized he had it better in his father's house, and decided to return home (Lu. 15:17). According to the Law of Moses, when the elders saw the son returning they could have stoned him.

However, the father (who depicts our loving, caring, sharing, heavenly Father) ran and fell upon his neck and kissed him (Lu. 15:20). The father's actions bespoke: *To get to my son you're going to have to stone me first.*

The overjoyed father instructed, *"Bring forth the best robe, and put it on him; and put a ring on his hand, and shoes on his feet: And bring hither the fatted calf...let us eat, and be merry"* (*vv. 22-23*). Then, the father called his neighbors and friends to celebrate that his lost son was found (vs. 24).

You may wonder why the father neglected to summon his oldest son. Well, you naturally anticipate, or at least hope the people of your own household would rejoice when your lost valuables are found. However, such was not the case with the elder brother.

Instead, when the elder brother arrived home and heard the music playing, he asked, *"What is going on?"* A servant responded, *"Your brother came home. Your father has ordered a feast—barbecued beef!—because he has him home safe and sound"* (Lu. 15:26-27 MSG).

The elder brother refused to rejoice at his younger brother's return. Instead, he displayed a bad attitude. Imagine if the elder brother had found him before the father did. Boy, that younger son would have been in serious trouble.

With a heart to console, the father went outside the party to find the eldest son sulking. Then the father explained: *"This is a wonderful time, and we had to celebrate. This brother of yours was dead, and he's alive! He was lost, and he's found (Lu. 15:32 MSG)!"* After that, the father returned to the party and left the elder son outside. We never know if the elder brother went in to rejoice.

However, we know heaven rejoices over one lost sinner that comes to Jesus Christ (Lu. 15:7). In Luke chapter 15, Jesus used these three parables to teach the subject of *lost and found*. Those of us that were lost should be excited because God loved us enough that He saved and redeemed us. We were lost and are now found!

GLORIFYING GOD THROUGH STEWARDSHIP

Love is the foundation and motivation for every manifestation of God's gifts to us. Moreover, our love for Him should be the motivation for whatever we do.

If we are going to glorify Him through our stewardship, we must come to understand 3 major points:

1. **The purpose of living**—*To glorify God*
2. **The principle of giving**—*To establish our living*
3. **The pattern of receiving**—*To have an attitude of gratitude*

The Apostle Paul speaks on the purpose of living:

> *For ye are bought with a price: therefore glorify God in your body, and in your spirit, which are God's.*
> *(1 Corinthians 6:20)*

Some people live their entire lives and never understand the purpose for their existence.

Jesus gives us the account of a poor man named Lazarus, and a rich man who God blessed with a tremendous amount of wealth. However, the rich man never used his wealth for the glory of God. One day, the rich man died and lifted up his eyes in hell because he never understood the real fundamental purpose of his life (Lu. 16:20-31). In essence, he squandered his stewardship.

The words *"steward"* and *"stewardship"* in the original Greek dialect is the word *"oikonomeo,"* which precedes from the Greek word *oikonomos*. Oikonomos is synonymous with our English word *"economy." Oikos* means *"house"* and *"nomos"* means law. In its proper context it means, *"the law of the house."*

There are all kinds of stewards in this world. True stewardship connotes *one entrusted with the belongings, possessions, and prosperity of another for the profitability of the owner.* Stewardship depends on the use of God-given blessings. The

God-given blessings are everything life consists of, namely; time, talents, gifts, possessions, and money.

When God made and formed man, He created everything man needed to function. He gave man breath and time began to tick–tock. Therefore, we are here on borrowed time. God loans time, talents, gifts, possessions, and money to see if we will use them for His glory.

It is evil to live on God's planet, breath God's air, and to leave God out of our lives. Sometimes we hear people say, *"I've got a place in my life for God."* However, it is important to note that God does not want a *place, but the place, the preeminence; 1st place is God's place.*

When Moses came down from Mt. Sinai with the Ten Commandments, the first command he quoted was *"Thou shall have no other gods before me."* God wants *first place*; **God must have preeminence!**

GLORIFYING GOD YIELDS THE "REST" OF GOD

Nothing can take the place of God; and lasting satisfaction is impossible without Jesus Christ. Truth is; glorifying God brings the rest of God.

> *Come unto me, all ye that labour and are heavy laden, and I will give you rest. Take my yoke upon you, and learn of me; for I am meek and lowly in heart: and ye shall find rest unto your souls. (Matthew 11:28-29)*

Notice in this verse Jesus said, *"Come."* He will always tell us to come because it is an act of our will. Jesus did not say, *"Come unto me all you that have a job."* He is not talking about physical work. He is speaking of labor as a part of living.

When Jesus bids those who are heavy laden to come to Him, He is not saying we will not experience stress, struggle, and strain. He is offering an exchange of rest and freedom from the stress, struggle, and strain of life.

Many verses in the Bible begin with, *"It came to pass."* At some point, the storm passes over. However, some people have pain throughout their lives. It is as though their stress, struggle, and strain *come to stay.*

Jesus tells us in verse 28 of Matthew 11, *"I will give you rest"* and then in verse 29 He says *"Ye shall find rest..."* Jesus gives us the first rest, and if we receive it, we find enjoyment, excitement, and fulfillment in the second rest. These rests come when we lean on Jesus.

In order to enjoy the benefits of His rest, we must become profitable stewards. Profitable stewards glorify God with their time, talents, gifts, possessions, and their money. For sake of differentiation, let's consider the unprofitable servant.

THE UNPROFITABLE SERVANT

In Luke chapter 15, Jesus expounded on lost and found. In Luke chapter 16, His teaching hinged upon being *lost forever.*

> *And he said also unto his disciples. There was a certain rich man, which had a steward; and the same was accused unto him that he had wasted his goods. And he called him, and said unto him, How is it that I hear this of thee? Give an account of thy stewardship; for thou mayest be no longer steward. (Luke 16:1-2)*

Jesus was teaching on the subject of stewardship. The overarching theme was a steward should be profitable.

Jesus was not so spiritually minded that He was no earthly good. Some relent and say, *"All Jesus ever thinks about is Heaven."* This is not true; Jesus wants us to prosper, so He speaks to us about everyday life situations. The illustration given about the unjust steward is one of them. Jesus is showing us through this parable how God judges a situation when we do not glorify Him.

The servant in question had never had the revelation of being a good steward. He was about to lose his job because he was not profitable to his boss. After all, what sensible boss would retain somebody who did not profit the business? Remember, stewards are over that which belongs to another person, and they are expected to gain profit for the owner. This servant didn't turn a profit and in the process of time, the boss found the man to be a poor steward over his resources.

> *Then the steward said within himself, What shall I do? For my lord taketh away from me the steward-ship: I cannot dig; to beg I am ashamed. (Luke 16:3)*

Understand, the unjust steward didn't say, *"I cannot dig"* because of a physical ailment that prevented him from dig-ging, he was just too lazy to work. Suddenly, the lights came on, and he said, *"I am resolved what to do, that, when I am put out of the stewardship, they may receive me into their houses (Luke 16:4)."*

> *So he called every one of his lord's debtors unto him, and said unto the first, How much owest thou unto my lord? And he said, An hundred measures of oil. And he said unto him, Take thy bill, and sit down quickly, and write fifty. Then said he to*

another, And how much owest thou? And he said,
An hundred measures of wheat. And he said unto him,
Take thy bill, and write fourscore. (Luke 16: 5-7)

Through deception, the servant decided to make friends with those indebted to his boss. He plotted so when he lost his job, those in debt would think, *"He lost his job because he gave me a break."* But, in reality, he had already lost his job. This shifty operator was just seeking whom he could con next.

Notice that the unjust steward asked the debtors, *"How much do you owe my lord?"* I find it rather disturbing this trifling man did not even know how much money the debtors owed his boss. After all, he was in charge of keeping the books.

One debtor owed one hundred measures of oil, or 100% of what he borrowed which is indicative that the employee never collected any of it or it was never recorded. He failed to do the job his master entrusted to his care. That might suggest this steward was involved with pilfering or embezzling his boss's profits the whole time. Is there any wonder this employee was found unprofitable?

> *And the lord commended the unjust steward,*
> *because he had done wisely: for the children*
> *of this world are in their generation wiser*
> *than the children of light. (Luke 16:8)*

Notice, the lord commended the unjust steward for his malicious activities. Bear in mind this was not the Lord, Jesus Christ who is commending the unjust steward; it was the man's boss. The commendation given here was not drawn from godly wisdom; it was and is the wisdom of this world. Concerning earthly wisdom, James the Apostle said, *"This wisdom descendeth not from above, but is earthly, sensual, devilish" (Jam. 3:15).*

The way of the world is sly, slick and wicked; it is about scheming, and doing things under the table. The unjust steward was slick and sly, and knew how to operate according to this world's system.

Jesus, speaking of the Father said, *"...I do always those things that please him (John 8:29)."* Sadly, like the unjust steward, many are looking to please themselves. Love for the Father was always Jesus' motivation. And, the motivation of our hearts and lives should be to please Him, also.

We are the children of light, but some still operate in darkness. Many operate under the table; doing the same old things they did in the world. Not only are there some unscrupulous people in the pews, but in the pulpit as well.

PROFITABLE STEWARDS TRUST GOD NOT MONEY

Jesus expressed trust in anything other than the person and power of the Lord Jesus Christ will fail (Lu. 16:9). Hence, dependency upon our government, family or finances will eventually result in disappointment. However, we are not disappointed when we trust Jesus; and our trust is revealed through how we handle our money.

> *He that is faithful in that which is least is faithful also in much: and he that is unjust in the least is unjust also in much. If therefore ye have not been faithful in the unrighteous mammon, who will commit to your trust the true riches? And if ye have not been faithful*

in that which is another man's, who shall give you that which is your own? No servant can serve two masters: for either he will hate the one, and love the other; or else he will hold to the one, and despise the other. Ye cannot serve God and mammon. (Luke 16:10-13)

If we are not faithful with money, we will not be faithful with anything else. According to 1 Corinthians 4:2, a steward must be found faithful. Faithfulness is what God **desires**, **admires**, and **requires**.

Our American currency is inscribed **"In God we trust."** Therefore, we must trust God, and not allow money to master our lives.

Judas allowed money to master him and was proven untrustworthy in ministry. He loved money so much that he stole from the treasury. Ultimately, he despised and betrayed Jesus for thirty pieces of silver. Ironically, when he received the silver, he did not want to spend it. In fact, he tried to give it back because he was dissatisfied.

True satisfaction comes when we trust the Lord with every aspect of our lives, especially our finances. As profitable stewards, when we are able to trust Him with money, we can attack our lack.

PROFITABLE STEWARDS ATTACK THEIR LACK

The way we attack our lack is by *giving what we need*, or *what we want to receive*. The world's system is designed to keep us down, and why wouldn't it be? Our enemy, the devil wants to depress and keeps us from listening to preachers who talk about money. The adversary does not mind preachers talking about Heaven. The plot is to prohibit them from talking about money.

The devil tries to trick people into believing all preachers are out to get their hands on money. Now, there are charlatans in the pulpit with motives for money. Nevertheless, there are true preachers assigned by God to get money to you. 2 Chronicles 20:20 says, *"...Believe in the Lord your God, so shall ye be established; believe his prophets [or pastors], so shall ye prosper"* *(parenthesis added)*.

To prosper means *to do better* and this is what God wants for His people. The Lord has given preachers to facilitate people in reaching that goal. God said, *"... I will give you pastors according to mine heart, which shall feed you with knowledge and understanding"* *(Jer. 3:15)*.

The pastor helps us multiply and increase in our lives through the anointing that removes burdens and destroys yokes. Jesus said, *"The Spirit of the Lord is upon me, because he hath anointed me to preach the gospel to the poor..."* *(Lu. 4:18)*.

America is supposedly the richest country in the world, so why are so many impoverished? Not only in America, but wherever you go; poverty is a reality because it is systemic. Poverty is designed to keep certain people down.

Many times, people of God describe themselves as being on a "fixed" income. That's okay. God wants us on a "fixed" income, He wants to fix it. Stop looking to the hand of man— look to the hand of God.

> *But my God shall supply all your need according to*
> *his riches in glory by Christ Jesus. (Philippians 4:19)*

God wants us to be poor no more.

God will use others to monetarily bless the poor. The problem is, often the poor do not know what to do with money. To many people money is viewed as a **need**, but it is a **seed**. The blessing is not in *the need*; it is in *the seed*. If you do not sow seed, you will always need. Jesus says, *"It is more blessed to give than to receive" (Acts 20:35)*. Giving breaks the back of poverty and meets every need.

Everyone should trust God, and glorify Him through stewardship. After all, this is our purpose in life.

CHAPTER TWO
QUESTIONS FOR REFLECTIONS

How would you describe your relationship with God?
Are you lost or found and why do you feel this way?

....

....

....

....

....

....

What are the three major points you need to know
in order to glorify God through stewardship?

1. ....

2. ....

3. ....

What are the God-given blessings that
everything in life consists of?

1. ....

2. ....

3. ....

4. ....

5. ....

There is a difference between an unjust and a profitable
steward. Are you unjust or profitable and why?

....

....

....

....

....

Why does the devil *not* want preachers to talk about money?

....

....

....

....

....

....

....

What does the word prosper mean?

Are you prospering? If you are, how?

....

....

....

....

....

....

....

3

SPENDING AND INVESTING IN LIVING

What? know ye not that your body is the temple of the Holy Ghost which is in you, which ye have of God, and ye are not your own? For ye are bought with a price: therefore glorify God in your body, and in your spirit, which are God's. (1 Corinthians 6:19-20)

IN THE AFOREMENTIONED SCRIPTURE, we are reminded we are not our own. The scripture also conveys the reason we were created and bought with a price. In other words, the Father made an investment in us through redemption. He did not redeem us with the blood of bulls and goats; we have been purchased by the blood of the Lamb—Jesus Christ.

Jesus spent everything when He died for our salvation. His spending was and is a sound investment. The word "spending" carries the connotation of *paying out, putting out* and *giving out*. Therefore, it is encumbered upon us to spend our lives for Him.

Whatever we do for Jesus is considered an investment. Some people spend their time, talents, gifts, possessions and money for personal gain. We must not waste our lives, but make the quality investment to live for God. Living for Him means being faithful stewards.

> *Moreover it is required in stewards, that a*
> *man be found faithful. (1 Corinthians 4:2)*

The qualification of a steward is faithfulness. God *admires* and *desires* faithfulness. Even more, He *requires* it. Stewardship consists of these five aspects:

1. **Time**
2. **Talents**
3. **Gifts**
4. **Possessions**
5. **Money**

We must spend and invest our time, talents, gifts, possessions, and money to glorify God. We will never be completely satisfied unless we glorify Him. **When we glorify God, He satisfies us.** Only God can and will be our true satisfaction—nobody can take His place, because He has preeminence (Col. 1:18).

OUR ACTION—MAKING THE BEST INVESTMENT

> *For ye are bought with a price: therefore glorify God in*
> *your body, and in your spirit, which are God's.*
> *(1 Corinthians 6:20)*

We make the best investment when we glorify God in our body and spirit. Someone may ask, *"What about our soul?"* The soul is the middleman. The soul always seeks to please itself. The devil captures us *when the soul is given control.*

Satan tried to snare Jesus by suggesting, *"Fall down and worship me (Matt. 4:9)."* When he says, *"Worship me,"* he's not only referring to himself; he'll settle for self-worship. If everything in life is about "self," the devil is gaining the advantage. He attempts to manipulate all of us into having a "me-ism" attitude.

Glorifying God is the best investment we can ever make. When we **glorify** Him, other people will **gain**, and it's for our **growth**. Usually adults make investments while children merely consume. Likewise, some Christians never make the proper investment and remain in an infantile state. Little children think only of themselves. Their mantra is, *"It's all about me!"* A child is not thinking about the parents, siblings or anyone else. Conversely, mature Christians don't seek self-glorification, but rather to glorify God. And, all things will works together for the **good** (Rom. 8:28).

Concerning our activities Paul said, *"Don't let it be done through strife or vain glory."* He revealed we can do things for our own glory. If it is not for God's glory; it's vainglory.

Let God be true and every man a liar (Rom. 3:4). We can operate in the name of God and yet not for His glory. Often, people get offended or hurt and leave the church; they disqualify themselves by operating for their own glory; not God's—that's a bad investment.

The church is the vehicle through which we make our most sound investments. God has churches and pastors everywhere. Elijah was looking to disconnect from the mission God had given him. He thought all of God's people were either gone or turned bad. Therefore, Elijah declared he was the only one left serving the Lord (1 Ki. 19:10). However, God replied that He had seven thousand faithful followers.

When things didn't go the way Elijah expected he withdrew himself from God's work. In light of Elijah's account, we must be careful not to think of ourselves more highly than we ought. Pride can hinder our faith, ultimately stifling our investment.

Some say, *"The church uses all of your time."* Let me borrow from songwriter Bill Withers who sang, *"I'm going to spread the news, if it feels this good to be used; keep on using me, until you use me up."* When the Lord is able to use us up we're making the best investment.

> *Examine yourselves, whether ye be in the faith;*
> *prove your own selves. Know ye not your own*
> *selves, how that Jesus Christ is in you, except*
> *ye be reprobates? (2 Corinthians 13:5)*

The term reprobate connotes *being rejected after testing*. God proves our deeds to show our motives. The test will reveal whether our actions are for vainglory or His glory. When we can complement and not compete in the church an investment is being made.

The Bible instructs us not to compare ourselves by ourselves that is not God's wisdom (2 Cor. 10:12). It also reminds us, we are workers together with Him (2 Cor. 6:1). Therefore, it is not **me-ism** it's **we-ism**. We are in this together to make the best investment.

INVESTING IN THE TREASURE

What in heaven do you have to show for your toil on earth? Many complain: *"I've worked, and have nothing to show for it."* Others have all of their treasures here on earth and absolutely nothing laid up for themselves in heaven.

Lay not up for yourselves treasures upon earth,
where moth and rust doth corrupt, and where
thieves break through and steal... (Matthew 6:19)

But lay up for yourselves treasures in heaven,
where neither moth nor rust doth corrupt, and
where thieves do not break through nor steal...
(Matthew 6:20)

Which one of the previous admonishments from Scripture do you regard? Do you lay up for yourself or not? We are to lay up treasures; however, they must be heavenly treasures. To further appreciate this concept let's consider the word treasure.

The word treasure is the Greek word *"thesaurus."* A thesaurus provides synonyms and antonyms for words. Therefore, when Jesus used the word treasure He was referring to a storehouse of knowledge and understanding.

Jesus saith unto them, Have ye understood all
these things? They say unto him, Yea, Lord.
Then said he unto them, Therefore every
scribe which is instructed unto the kingdom
of heaven is like unto a man that is an house-
holder, which bringeth forth out of his treasure
things new and old. (Matthew 13:51-52)

Jesus asked His disciples, *"Do you understand, and have you understood these things?"* They said unto Him, *"Yea Lord."* Jesus began His next thought with, *"Every scribe..."* We become a scribe of what we are taught. A scribe is a teacher of Kingdom life. In essence, Jesus was asking if they understood Kingdom life.

For the sake of making a point, let's look at a heart special-ist who performs heart surgery. This person could have grad-uated top of their class and possess all the book knowledge; however, the questions remain, *"Do they have any experience in heart surgery? How many open-heart surgeries have they performed?"* This person could have a plethora of knowledge in their head, but no experience in their hands.

Some people have spiritual knowledge, but no experience with God. Thus, they can become reprobates; *rejected after testing*. We have to pass the test. Our understanding allows us to become teachers of what Jesus taught and investors into the Kingdom's treasures.

OUR AMBITION—LIVING MY LIFE AS AN INVESTMENT

> *For where your treasure is, there will your heart be also. The light of the body is the eye: if therefore thine eye be single, thy whole body shall be full of light. But if thine eye be evil... (Matthew 6:21-23)*

We can live as an investment to God. Jesus does not want us to live evil, but good lives. The word evil is the word live spelled backward. This helps us understand that evil living is backward living or living without God. If we leave God out of the equation of our lives, that is evil.

Although Jesus did not mention being wicked, we must deal with wickedness. Wickedness is pretending to be righ-teous and underneath the facade being treacherous. God's true sheep can be subject to sin, but are not wicked. Nevertheless, a wolf in sheep's clothing is wicked.

> *Wherefore the Lord said, Forasmuch as this*
> *people draw near me with their mouth, and*
> *with their lips do honor me, but have removed*
> *their heart far from me... (Isaiah 29:13)*

We must not come to the house of God to merely spend time; we must come to make an investment. Unfortunately, everybody that comes to church is not coming for the right reason. There are people in church operating in witchcraft. Manasseh ruled over Judah as king and built altars to idols in God's house, which was evil in the sight of the Lord.

> *And he caused his children to pass through the fire*
> *in the valley of the son of Hinnom: also he observed*
> *times, and used enchantments, and used witchcraft,*
> *and dealt with a familiar spirit, and with wizards:*
> *he wrought much evil in the sight of the LORD,*
> *to provoke him to anger. (2 Chronicles 33:6)*

By laying up treasure in heaven and being righteous, our lives are investments for the Kingdom. Treasure can be defined as *the grabber of our attention and the motivator of our heart.* Jesus must be our Treasure, thereby the reason why we *pay out, put out* and *give out.*

When I visited Germany I had to convert my American currency. When people come from different nations, they have to convert their currency to ours. Money is not the same everywhere you go. A dollar does not carry the same value in every nation. A dollar does not carry the same value it once did in America. Just as the operation of conversion in currency goes, we must convert God's blessings from **vainglory** to **His glory**—this is a good investment.

For who maketh thee to differ from another? And
what hast thou that thou didst not receive? Now
if thou didst receive it, why dost thou glory, as if
thou hadst not received it? (1 Corinthians 4:7)

Paul said whatever we have God gave it to us. Remember, all that we do should be for God's **glory**, other peoples' **gain**, and our **growth**.

An invested life is one that is used to redeem others. We make deposits into our investment when people are delivered from a life of darkness. The only things we take to heaven are our testimonies and the souls of people we help deliver.

An invested life is one that gives. I trust like me you live to give. The Jesus in me is the giver in me, and my broke days are over. We should look to be a blessing to others and not merely eke out a living. God says, *"Prove Me" (Mal. 3:10).* Don't test Him. By giving, we prove He blesses us coming in and going out; in the city and in the field. We don't have to rip people off or cheat. God will make us the head and not the tail.

We don't have to serve the devil to drive the best, wear the finest or live the highest. As our lives are invested in God's kingdom, He meets our every need (Phil. 4:19).

OUR ATTITUDE—LIFE INVESTMENT GONE BAD

And one of the company said unto him, Master,
speak to my brother, that he divide the inheritance
with me. And he said unto him, Man, who made
me a judge or a divider over you?... And he spake a
parable unto them, saying, The ground of a certain

rich man brought forth plentifully: And he thought (attitude), saying, What shall I do, because I have no room where to bestow my fruits? And he said, This will I do: (action) I will pull down my barns, and build greater; and there will I bestow all my fruits and my goods. And I will say to my soul... (ambition). (Luke 12:13-19 bold words and parenthesis added)

The man in the aforementioned text gives an example of a life investment gone badly. His investment was squandered because of his attitude toward the treasures he possessed on the earth.

Through vain ambition; he amassed so much wealth he needed to make more room for it. However, his treasure was not invested in the kingdom of heaven, we know this because he said, *"And I will say to my soul."* The man never spoke with God; he conversed only with his soul. Again, the Scripture admonishes us to glorify God in our body and our spirit (1 Cor. 6:20).

...Soul, thou hast much goods laid up for many years; take thine ease, eat, drink, and be merry. (Luke 12:19)

This man, speaking to himself, decided to waste his life. Nevertheless, God said, *"Thou fool, this night thy soul shall be required of thee: then whose shall those things be, which thou hast provided"* (Lu. 12:20)? God considered this man a fool and further admonished, *"So is he that layeth up treasure for himself, and is not rich toward God"* (Lu. 12:21).

This man laid up treasure for himself and what happened? His soul was required that very night. I'm sure you've heard the saying, *"Here today; gone tomorrow."* This statement is not entirely true. The truth is, *"Here today; gone today.*" In other words, no one is promised tomorrow. All we have is today; therefore, we better make the right investment.

If you haven't already, make the decision to have a rich relationship toward God today. Whatever you do, don't just spend your time working to acquire earthly goods; invest your life by storing up treasure in heaven. The spiritual gifts you possess are God's gifts to you; using these gifts to glorify His name is your gift to Him—stop spending; start investing.

CHAPTER THREE
QUESTIONS FOR REFLECTIONS

Are you living for God? If you are, explain:

....

....

....

....

....

....

When you live for God it affects everyone.
God gets the .... ; others get the .... ;
you get the...and it all works together for the

....

How do you know when your actions are
for God's glory and not vain glory?

....

....

....

....

....

....

What is the difference between an evil
person and a wicked person?

....

....

....

....

....

....

Are you living an invested life? If so, explain? If you
are not living an invested life, how can you start?

....

....

....

....

....

....

Are you spending or investing your life
for God? Explain your answer.

....

....

....

....

....

....

....

....

....

....

....

....

....

....

....

....

....

....

THE PRINCIPLE OF GIVING

{SECTION II}

4

THE PRINCIPLE OF GIVING
POSSESSING YOUR POSSESSIONS

*But upon mount Zion shall be deliverance, and there shall be holiness; and the house of Jacob **shall possess their possessions**. And the house of Jacob shall be a fire, and the house of Joseph a flame, and the house of Esau for stubble, and they shall kindle in them, and devour them; and there shall not be any remaining of the house of Esau; for the LORD hath spoken it. (Obadiah 1:17-18 boldness added)*

THE PRINCIPLE OF GIVING establishes our living and it allows us to possess our possessions. In Scripture, Mount Zion is often used metaphorically to depict the church of the Living God. The Scripture reads, *"Upon mount Zion shall be deliverance."* This is to say our deliverance comes from the house of the Lord. Obadiah goes on to declare, *"There shall be holiness, and the house of Jacob shall possess their possessions."*

While the house of Jacob is delivered, the house of Esau will be for stubble and eventually devoured. There is a distinct difference between Jacob and Esau. Esau sold his birthright for a meal. The birthright was the inheritance reserved for the first born son and it was considered precious. However, Esau failed to see his inheritance as valuable. Hence, he relinquished his prized possessions to his brother.

We must view our position in Jesus Christ as a prized possession. Unlike Esau, we must value the Spirit of Christ within us. Jesus' very nature is giving. Therefore, as He is given preeminence in our lives, we become givers as well. Through *the principle of giving* we learn to receive what we need while breaking the back of greed.

BREAKING THE BACK OF GREED

And I will give you pastors according to mine heart, which shall feed you with knowledge and understanding. And it shall come to pass, when ye be multiplied and increased in the land... (Jeremiah 3:15-16)

Some people never give anything because of a greedy heart. This can cause them to go through life struggling without financial success. For this cause, God has given pastors to reveal His heart toward prosperity.

Although there has been a negative report about pastors who preach the Lord's prosperity, this is mandated by God. Many believe the pastor is out to get people's money, but the truth is, God-given pastors are out to get people money. In other words, these pastors teach people how to get money and prosper through the word of God. They teach the principle of giving establishes our living and breaks the back of greed and stinginess. This is a fixed principle of operation that leaves no room for negotiation, debate or discussion.

As a result of greed, Jacob ran from Esau because he acquired his brother's birthright by deception (Gen. 27:36).

While fleeing, he happened upon a particular place where he took rocks and made a pillow for himself. During his sleep Jacob had a dream of a ladder that went to heaven. The Lord stood at the top of the ladder, and when Jacob awakened, he said, *"This is none other but the house of God, and this is the gate of heaven" (Gen. 28:17).*

It was in this place that God communicated with Jacob. Jacob's name meant "supplanter" or "holder of the heel." All of his life Jacob was a schemer and dreamer coming up with ploys to fulfill his greed. Jacob's initial impulse was to conspire in order to get, but God wanted to teach him to give. Therefore, God showed Jacob His generosity first.

> *And, behold, I am with thee, and will keep thee in all places whither thou goest, and will bring thee again into this land; for I will not leave thee, until I have done that which I have spoken to thee of. (Genesis 28:15)*

Jacob had to come to a place where God's presence resided in order to make a change. He said this is the gate of heaven, and then connected it to the house of God. In that hallowed place the angels ascended and descended in the earth (Gen. 28:12).

Many people are struggling financially. For that reason, God has anointed His servants to preach the gospel to the poor (Lu. 4:18). If we are covenant-keeping people we are connected to a local church, and in the local church God has ordained a pastor to teach us that the poor do not have to be poor anymore.

Even though his father and his grandfather were rich, Jacob was poor. At first, he did not invest his life or money in the kingdom of God. He spent everything he had on selfish pursuits. Like Jacob, greed can cause us to think of self when we should think of God.

Jacob made a pivotal decision that literally broke the back of greed and cast the spirit of poverty from his life. He vowed a monetary vow to the Lord and above the vow he made a promise to tithe (Gen. 28:20-22).

When Jacob invested his life in the kingdom of God, God changed his name from Jacob to Israel (Gen. 32:27-28). He had nothing monetarily to give, but by faith he vowed a vow. *Beloved, you have nothing to lose if you have nothing to give.* If you are down to nothing financially, tap into spiritual success. Don't withdraw because of greed; give and trust God will meet your need. Like Jacob, vow a vow. Break the back of greed through the principle of giving.

We break the back of greed when we release our seed of faith. Releasing a seed of faith goes along with releasing money. Money is simply a method for measuring our faith. If you will not believe God by giving when you have a little money, you will not believe Him and give when you have much. Now, God is not looking at our money, He is considering our faith. This is why He instituted the vow system.

The vow is to help us break the back of greed. Therefore, it is imperative we understand the principle of the vow, which is:

- **Make a vow**

- As God gives to you; **pay on the vow until the vow is paid**.

- Once the vow is paid, **don't retreat (financially speaking)**. God never stops giving what He was giving during the vow.

- **Start tithing on what God is currently giving you**. Subsequently, God will trust you with more—and more—and more.

The vow allows us to get into God's river of blessings. His river flows and goes from our ankles to our knees; from our knees to our loins; from our loins to our chest and before you know it, we are swimming in God's abundant life (Eze. 47:1-5). This principle of giving establishes our living.

Just about everyone desires financial freedom and we all want to possess our possessions. Can you imagine living in the land of abundance? If so, you must be willing to give. God's Word declares: give and it shall be given back to you in a good measure, pressed down, shaken together and running over (Lu. 6:38). Now realize, if you cannot give there (in abundance), you cannot live there.

God wants His children to have the ability to see, take and keep. Some people are able to see what God desires for them, but can't take it. There are some who can see it and take it, but they cannot keep what God says is theirs. The only way we can see, take and keep is by understanding and applying the principle I am teaching. The principle of giving breaks the back of greed and allows the Lord to supply all that we need.

THE LORD LONGS TO GIVE

> *Now the LORD had said unto Abram, Get thee*
> *out of thy country, and from thy kindred, and*
> *from thy father's house, unto a land that I will*
> *shew thee: And I will make of thee a great nation,*
> *and I will bless thee, and make thy name great;*
> *and thou shalt be a blessing: (Genesis 12:1-2)*

The Lord longed to give and He wanted Abraham to learn this first hand. Therefore, God told Abraham to leave his father's house. Abraham and his wife Sarah obeyed God and followed Him by faith. The Lord instructed Abraham to trade his homeland for God's Promised Land.

God assured Abraham the land was flowing with milk and honey. However, Abraham arrived at the Promised Land only to discover a desert. The land showed no signs of production or prosperity. Notwithstanding, this place was the dirt and God had the seed to produce His harvest—Abraham was the seed.

You might be reading this book from a desert place in your life. You may wonder if God knows you're broke and barren. Beloved, God knows and He wants you to discover His promised land for your life. However, you must comprehend a promise is just that, a promise. This means the land is not going to produce the harvest until there is the principle of giving, or the sowing of seed. Like Abraham, you are the seed.

Abraham occupied the land and it became fruitful just as God promised. In every direction the land was prosperous. Abraham's nephew Lot prospered because of Abraham and Sarah's obedience. Everything and everybody associated with Abraham lived in abundance. In fact, the immense wealth caused tension within the camp.

> *And there was a strife between the herdmen of*
> *Abram's cattle and the herdmen of Lot's cattle..."*
> *"And Abram said unto Lot, Let there be no strife, I*
> *pray thee, between me and thee, and between my*
> *herdmen and thy herdmen; for we be brethren. Is not*
> *the whole land before thee? separate thyself, I pray*
> *thee, from me: if thou wilt take the left hand, then*

I will go to the right; or if thou depart to the right
hand, then I will go to the left. (Genesis 13:7-9)

The Lord gave Abraham, and Lot was a beneficiary of his uncle's blessings. While Abraham was giving God his life, Lot was living for his lust. The time had come when the two had to separate. Lot's greed and selfishness caused him to look at greener grass (Gen. 13:10). Lot could have suggested dividing what appeared to be the better land with Abraham, but he didn't. No, Lot wanted all of it. He wanted what he thought was the best. However, he was sadly mistaken.

Abraham followed God and in spite of appearances; he had the best because he had God's promise.

And the Lord said unto Abram, after that Lot was
separated from him, Lift up now thine eyes, and
look from the place where thou art northward,
and southward, and eastward, and westward: For
all the land which thou seest, to thee will I give
it, and to thy seed for ever. (Genesis 13:14-15)

Lot loss everything he possessed while God taught Abraham to possess his possessions and recover everything the enemy stole.

The following text is lengthy, but I believe it necessary to fully appreciate all the Lord gave Abraham. What's more, we are able to gain a proper perspective of Abraham's gratitude for the Lord's generosity.

And he brought back all the goods, and also brought
again his brother Lot, and his goods, and the women
also, and the people. And the king of Sodom went out
to meet him after his return from the slaughter of
Chedorlaomer, and of the kings that were with him,

at the valley of Shaveh, which is the king's dale. And Melchizedek king of Salem brought forth bread and wine: and he was the priest of the most high God. And he blessed him, and said, Blessed be Abram of the most high God, possessor of heaven and earth: And blessed be the most high God, which hath delivered thine enemies into thy hand. And he gave him tithes of all. And the king of Sodom said unto Abram, Give me the persons, and take the goods to thyself. And Abram said to the king of Sodom, I have lift up mine hand unto the Lord, the most high God, the possessor of heaven and earth, That I will not take from a thread even to a shoelatchet, and that I will not take any thing that is thine, lest thou shouldest say, I have made Abram rich: (Gen 14:16-23)

The Lord longs to give and so He gave Abraham victory over his enemies. Melchizedek the king of Salem represented God. He approached Abraham with the gifts of bread and wine. Did Melchizedek ask Abraham to give anything? No, he did not! Yet, Abraham understood the principle of giving and by that; he was able to possess his possessions. Since God blessed him with all those goods, Abraham gave tithes of all.

On the other hand, the king of Sodom represents the spirit of this world. This king didn't come to give, he came to take. He asked Abraham for the people he recovered from the enemies' hands and had the nerve to say Abraham could keep the goods.

Abraham said to the king of Sodom, I have lift up my hand to the Lord, the most-high God; the possessor of heaven and earth. In other words, he pledged and made a vow to God.

He lifted his hands because he knew God was his source. Abraham told this worldly king he wouldn't take anything; thereby, the king couldn't say, *"I have made Abraham rich."*

God is the possessor of heaven and earth. He wanted Abraham to be rich, but he did not want the riches to possess him. The Lord longs to give to you, but you must break the back of greed by giving to the Lord. Some may say, *"How much should I give to God?"* The focus is not on the *measure* of your giving, but the *motive*. Our giving should be indicative of our trust.

> *Ye that fear the LORD, trust in the LORD: he is*
> *their help and their shield. (Psalms 115:11)*

We must trust what God gives is for our benefit not detriment. When we are leaning on Jesus, we are trusting in the Lord. He is our help and our shield. He is our *satisfaction*, our *direction* and gives us *protection*.

> *The LORD hath been mindful of us: he will bless*
> *us; he will bless the house of Israel; he will bless the*
> *house of Aaron. He will bless them that fear the*
> *LORD, both small and great. (Psalms 115:12-13)*

The aforementioned scripture should be a comfort in your time of need. It declares the Lord is mindful of us; therefore, He will bless us. This is why I say, *"The Lord longs to give."* All day, every day you're on His heart. Not one minute goes by that He doesn't have your welfare in mind. Just as He blessed the house of Israel, He continues to bless your house. His blessings are not always packaged financially. He desires to give His peace; good health; fulfillment in your family and so much more.

The LORD shall increase you more and more,
you and your children. (Psalms 115:14)

It cannot be overstated, the Lord longs to give and His Word declares He shall increase you more and more, you and your children. Imagine that! God is thinking about your future and the future of your children. Don't rob your family of God's finest. The Lord longs to give; He loves to give; the question is—do you?

THE RICH AND THE KINGDOM OF GOD

It is easier for a camel to go through the
eye of a needle, than for a rich man to enter
into the kingdom of God. (Mark 10:25)

Whatever you do, don't allow riches to keep you from the kingdom of God.

There was a rich young ruler who called Jesus, good master, while inquiring about the way to eternal life (Mark 10:17). Jesus knowing the man's motives addressed him on the word good. Jesus asked the young ruler, *"Why callest thou me good? There is none good but one, that is, God" (Mark 10:18).*

Now, the man was facing a conundrum; he had to answer the question of Jesus' deity and his own piety. This ruler wasn't calling Jesus a good master because he thought Jesus was God; he merely wanted to be considered a good master himself. Therefore, Jesus moved beyond flattery and tackled the root of the issue—this man's ego.

At some point we all do well and are morally good because Jesus dwells within us. Conversely, if God is not internally dwelling in us we can do a whole lot of good, but that does not make us good. Many people perform a lot of good because they have ulterior motives; it's called "vainglory" (Gal. 5:26). They are performing for their own gain and glamour.

In order to possess our possessions we must know the purpose of living is to magnify God. We must call Jesus good on the bases of His deity, period. There must be no hidden agenda on our parts; we must crown Jesus Lord over our lives. The rich young ruler enquired the way to eternal life and Jesus didn't mince words.

> *Thou knowest the commandments, Do not*
> *commit adultery, Do not kill, Do not steal, Do*
> *not bear false witness, Defraud not, Honour*
> *thy father and mother. (Mark 10:19)*

While Jesus was rehearsing the commandments in the ruler's ears, the young man interrupted: *"Master, all these have I observed from my youth" (Mark 10:20)*. Jesus' response gives insight to the love of God for all people.

> *Then Jesus beholding him loved him, and said*
> *unto him, One thing thou lackest: go thy way, sell*
> *whatsoever thou hast, and give to the poor, and*
> *thou shalt have treasure in heaven: and come,*
> *take up the cross, and follow me. (Mark 10:21)*

The man was border-lining obnoxiousness, but Jesus didn't scold him; Jesus beheld him. Jesus looked at him and loved him. Jesus gave the ruler instructions not from a place of contempt; but from a place of concern.

The Lord revealed this man had chosen the wrong god. The ruler called Jesus good master, but in reality he made money his master.

Jesus told him that he lacked one thing. The one thing this man lacked was the very first commandment: *"Thou shalt have no other gods before me" (Ex. 20:3).* Therefore, Jesus told him the way to eternal life was to sell everything he had. God wanted to show the only way to break the back of greed was through the *principle of giving.*

Furthermore, once the ruler sold everything he had, he was instructed to give it all to the poor. Only then would he have treasures in heaven. Apparently, this man's treasure was not in heaven, it was in the earth. Jesus asked him to take up the cross, which is the cause of God, for the glory of God. He told him, *"Take up the cross and follow me" (Mark 10:21).* The man did not have the cross in mind nor the glory of God. He was certainly not ready to follow the Lord. He was following and pursuing his own money.

At this point I want to explain the problems with making money our master. First there's the **"description of a difficulty."** The description is that the treasures on earth, no matter what or where it is, will not last forever. Everything on earth decays; nothing will last (Matt. 6:19).

Similarly, you might not last to enjoy it. You can put all your money in the bank and suddenly die before you can enjoy it. Material things will not last, and you may not last to enjoy them. Jesus described the difficulty by saying, *in the end you cannot take it in.*

In the end, you can request all your belongings be placed in the grave with you and that is where they'll stay. You cannot take them to heaven. However, you can take your testimony and the souls of people who were saved because of your investment.

The second problem with money as a master is the

"creation of the danger." This means you become what you pursue. The Bible says about Judas, *"He was a thief, and since he was in charge of the disciples' money, he often stole some for himself"* *(John 12:6 NLT)*. Judas, as the treasurer among Jesus' disciples had the moneybag and he was stealing out of it. Judas was a liar and a thief, which caused him to become a traitor.

After Jesus revealed the way to eternal life was through the principle of giving, the Bible records concerning the rich ruler: *"And he was sad at that saying, and went away grieved: for he had great possessions"* *(Mark 10:22)*.

Just think; the young ruler should have been glad that Jesus revealed the way to eternal life, but he walked away sad. He went away grieved (Mark 10:22). He was sad, hurting, and walked away as if a death had occurred. He knew he was not going to heaven and therefore grieved at his own figurative funeral. He grieved because he had great possessions. Moreover, his possessions possessed him.

If we are to avoid the description of a difficulty and the creation of a danger, we can't allow money to master us; we must master our money by placing God first and giving Jesus the preeminence. It is vital that we follow Jesus in order to possess our possessions. We must go after Him and not after things.

CHAPTER FOUR
QUESTIONS FOR REFLECTION

How do you view your position with Jesus Christ?

....
....
....
....
....

Does your pastor teach the principle of living?
If so, how does it affect your life?

....
....
....
....
....

According to this chapter, how are you able to
break the back of greed in your life?

....
....
....
....
....

Explain the principle of the vow.

....
....
....
....
....

What does the principle of giving allow you to do? Are you
operating from this principle in your life? If so, explain:

....

....

....

....

....

....

What are the two primary problems with
making money our master?

Describe these two problems.

1. ....

....

....

....

....

....

....

2. ....

....

....

....

....

....

....

....

5

HOW YOU VIEW GOD

The light of the body is the eye: if therefore thine eye be single, thy whole body shall be full of light. But if thine eye be evil, thy whole body shall be full of darkness. If therefore the light that is in thee be darkness, how great is that darkness! No man can serve two masters: for either he will hate the one, and love the other; or else he will hold to the one, and despise the other. Ye cannot serve God and mammon. (Matthew 6:22-24)

ARE YOU A SINGLE or evil-eyed Christian? God wants us to see Him as He is, that is either with a single eye or through an evil eye. There is no in between. Jesus says if we are luke-warm He will spew us out of His mouth (Rev. 3:16)! We must be hot or cold, up or down, in or out, single-eyed or evil-eyed.

Everything in the Bible is given through a revelation of a difference. This means a distinction is made about objects and subjects based upon our revelation. For instance, the word **live** spelled backwards is the word **evil**. By this we come to understand evil is living backwards or leaving God out of the equation of our lives.

There is a revelation of a difference between an evil person and a wicked person. A person can be a sinner and still not be wicked. On the other hand, a person can pretend to be saved, this is wicked. A wicked person gives the impression of following God, but all the time they are not. This person is phony and hypocritical. Jesus called the Pharisees hypocrites because they put on righteousness with deception (Matt. 6:1-24).

OUR VIEW MAKES THE DIFFERENCE

How do you view God? Do you view Him as He should be viewed? This is one of the questions Jesus asked His disciples. In Matthew 16:15, Jesus says, *"...Who do you say I am?"* How do you view Him? Do you see Jesus as the Son of God? If you cannot see Him the way you should, you will have an identity crisis. It is not who you say you are; it is not who I say I am. It is who God says we are. ***Our identity is with Divinity.***

God is the master Architect and He is building each of us. We are the house in which Jesus abides. Jesus dwells in us, thus our identity is in Him.

The writer of Hebrews 3:1-4 says:

> *Wherefore, holy brethren, partakers of the heavenly calling, consider the Apostle and High Priest of our profession, Christ Jesus; Who was faithful to him that appointed him, as also Moses was faithful in all his house. For this man was counted worthy of more glory than Moses, inasmuch as he who hath builded the house hath more honor than the house. For every house is builded by some man; but he that built all things is God.*

We are the house of God. The Bible says to us, *"What? know ye not that your body is the temple of the Holy Ghost which is in you, which ye have of God, and ye are not your own" (1 Cor. 6:19)?* Our body is the temple of the Holy Spirit and ultimately Jesus'.

Do we manage our lives the way God says we should? Do we operate the way God says? How does this apply to our house (life)? The Lord is not talking about the house that we live in; He speaks of His dwelling place (our temple or our body).

Do we really treasure what we have in the Lord? If we view God correctly, we see Him dwelling on the inside of us. Therefore, the proper perspective causes us to operate according to His Word.

We know the price for just about everything and anything in the world; but at the same time we fail to know the treasure we have in the Kingdom. *Money* is least in the kingdom of God. Yet *money* is of the highest value in the world. We are stewards and our stewardship begins with our view of God and His kingdom.

It is imperative for us to understand how we should view God; single-eyed. To have a single eye means we pursue Jesus. In the pursuit of Him, nothing should distract us. There are Ten Kingdom Keys of Maturity and I would like to reference two of them. The first key is, *"The level of a man or woman's maturity is their ability to hear from God, step out by faith and obey what God says" (Jam. 1:22-23).* The eighth key is, *"The level of a man or woman's maturity is their ability to keep their focus on their purpose and stay in the positive lane" (Acts 20:24; 1 Thess. 5:18).* We are to keep our focus on our purpose, which is to glorify God through stewardship.

Some may say, *"I can't see Jesus."* However, the only way to view Him is with a single eye. The purpose of our living is to pursue Him, go after Him, seek Him, chase Him and hunt for Him. It's all about Him! The same way we hunt for treasure, we are to hunt for the Lord Jesus Christ and love Him with all of our heart (Matt. 22:37).

Jesus declares, *"But seek ye first the kingdom of God..."* *(Matt. 6:33)*. God's kingdom comes first and there is no second. If there was a second, it would be just as important as the first. In others words, if we say number 1 then that means there has to be number 2, 3, 4, etc. The simplicity of being single-eyed means Jesus is first and only, there are no seconds and so forth.

When Jesus is given preeminence, God will add to our lives. He wants us to have the best. He is our Creator. When He created Adam and Eve the only thing they had to do was take care of what God had provided and planted in the Garden (Gen. 2:8,15). God knows when to give us what we need and He wants to give it to us.

> But seek ye first the kingdom of God, and his
> righteousness; and all these things shall be
> added unto you. Take therefore no thought for
> the morrow: for the morrow shall take thought
> for the things of itself. Sufficient unto the day
> is the evil thereof. (Mathew 6:33-34)

If we view the Lord correctly, and keep our eyes single on Him, everything we need will be given to us. It does not matter if it is a car, a house, a husband or a wife, if we pursue Jesus, *"all these things"* will be added to us. We just need to have the right view because our view makes all the difference.

VIEWING GOD IN OUR GIVING

We must operate in the principle of giving. A principle is *a fixed law of operation that leaves no room for negotiation, debate, or discussion.* We'll have no problem giving when we view God properly.

God so loved the world that He gave... (John 3:16). Therefore, it is crucial that we understand the principle of giving. The only thing that can break the back of greed and stinginess is *giving.* God wants us to break greed and stinginess from our lives. If we are not givers, we are not viewing God the way we should. Hence, *the more we give, the more He gives to us.*

Some people take what the preacher says lightly. They despise what they hear from the Word of God. The word *despise* in Matthew 6:24 in the original Greek is translated as "kataphroneo." This carries the meaning of *"to think down, low, little or light."* It is a take-it-or-leave-it kind of spirit and attitude.

In Matthew 6:24, God is telling us, *"No man can serve two masters: for either he will hate the one, and love the other; or else he will hold to the one, and despise the other..."* The choice is clear. A man serves either God or things of the world.

In Luke 12:15 Jesus said unto them, *"Take heed, and beware of covetousness..."* which is greed and stinginess. Stinginess causes us to clinch our fists tightly. However, God desires that we open our hands, because He cannot put money into fists. Never forget, our giving establishes our living. It is important to understand ***if we cannot give there*** (in abundance) ***we cannot live there.***

Jesus taught His disciples about covetousness, which is greed and stinginess. In Luke 12:13 the Bible says, *"And one of the company said unto him, Master, speak to my brother, that he divide the inheritance with me."*

To this request Jesus replied, *"Man who made me a judge or a divider over you"* (v. 14). Then Jesus said, *"Take heed, and beware of covetousness: for a man's life consisteth not in the abundance of the things which he possesseth"* (v. 15).

A person's life consists of his perspectives. This is why we must view God correctly even in our giving. **God has never been opposed to us having things, but He is opposed to things having us**.

As we look further into Luke chapter 12, Jesus also shared the account of a man who tore down his barns and built more barns because of his greed. This man built new barns to store his goods and live like a king. The man said to himself, *"Soul, thou hast much goods laid up for many years; take thine ease, eat, drink, and be merry"* (Lu. 12:19). This man failed to view God in his giving. He poured all his wealth on himself.

God responded to the man's actions by saying, *"Thou fool, this night thy soul shall be required of thee: then whose shall those things be, which thou hast provided"* (Lu. 12:20)? His time had run out. Now, who is going to get all that stuff in his barns? Jesus stated, we should not lay up treasures for ourselves, but rather be rich toward God (Lu. 12:21). We are rich toward God only when we serve Him in our giving.

In Matthew 6:24 Jesus says we cannot serve God and mammon. He did not say we could not serve God and the devil because no one following God willingly serves the devil. The emphasis that Jesus made was we cannot serve God and mammon. Mammon is a common Arabic word which deals with *material wealth*; and here it was personified as an *object of worship*.

Money can be, and is to be, a thermometer to measure the heat of our commitment to God. Money locates our hearts. Jesus says, *"For where your treasure is, there your heart will be also" (Matt. 6:21).*

This is certainly not a put down on anybody but some people have taken vows and dedicated themselves to a life of poverty. However, this is not what God is suggesting (Matt. 6:24). God wants us to enjoy life and not allow mammon (money) to be a controlling force over us.

We must choose a master, because no one can serve two. We will serve one or the other. When we view God in our giving the choice is quite clear.

CHANGE OUR VIEW; CHANGE OURSELVES

Let's further discuss the importance of having a single-eyed view of God. If our eye is single we're pursuing God; we become more like Him, displaying godliness.

The word godliness in the original Greek is "eusebeia." This Greek term means *"to be devout,"* and denotes that which is characterized by a Godward attitude, or one who does that which is well-pleasing to God.

If we are not going after God then we become unlike Him, *"worldly."* We are either *godly* or *worldly.* Our view of God is critical in our developmental process. If we see God positively and we know that He's acting with our best interest in mind, we will think and behave positively. Conversely, if we see God negatively or believe Him to be inadequate, we will behave in accordance to our belief. In short, ***change your view; change yourself.***

> *But godliness with contentment is
> great gain. (1 Timothy 6:6)*

We must view God as our source. And as our source we must know He is adequate. God lacks nothing. *He does not only give us what we need, He is who we need.* Armed with this knowledge should provide us with certain contentment.

Contentment is *an uncomplaining acceptance of my own lot.* The only way we can be fulfilled and totally satisfied is by the Lord Jesus Christ. He alone can satisfy us and add all the things we need for certain success (Matt. 6:33). He is the **Good Shepherd** (John10:11), **Great Shepherd** (Heb. 13:20), **Chief Shepherd** (1 Pet. 5:4) therefore, all we like sheep (Isa. 53:6) need the Shepherd.

We are called the sheep of our Lord and not goats. If sheep do not have a shepherd, they will wander off. On the other hand, goats butt everything, *"I hear what the Shepherd is saying but...."* Sheep have a way of wandering if there is no shepherd. Jesus is our Shepherd who leads us into green pastures (Ps. 23). He is taking us into the very best that He wants for us. If we don't pursue the Shepherd, then we are not becoming more like God, which is *godly*; we are becoming unlike God, which is *worldly.*

Again, godliness with contentment is an uncomplaining acceptance of my own lot. When we meet a Christian or somebody who is always murmuring, complaining, whining, crying, arguing, fussing, fighting, fretting, disobedient, rebellious and stubborn it is because they are not going after God. Their vision of God is skewed; and their behavior is reflective of their view. Everything is wrong because their view of God is wrong.

Some go after possessions without realizing the God who owns it all has the power to give it all. Many things distract them. When we are content in terms of what we have there is an uncomplaining acceptance of our own lot. We can rejoice with other people because we are satisfied.

> *And having food and raiment let us be therewith content. But they that will be rich fall into temptation and a snare, and into many foolish and hurtful lusts, which drown men in destruction and perdition. For the love of money is the root of all evil ... (1 Timothy 6:8-10)*

On the back of our U.S. currency it reads, "In God We Trust." For years I thought it was only printed on the one dollar bill (which is all I had). I later discovered "In God We Trust" was inscribed on every bill. It is God we trust, not the money.

Some people don't want money because they think it's evil. Paul didn't say money is the root of all evil. He simply stated to love money is evil. Like everything else, it comes down to how we view money and how we view God.

> *For the love of money is the root of all evil: which while some coveted after, they have erred from the faith, and pierced themselves through with many sorrows... Charge them that are rich in this world, that they be not high minded... (1 Timothy 6:10,17)*

God wants us rich in this world but not high-minded. He does not want us to think more highly than we ought to think about ourselves (Rom. 12:3). Our economic status (especially if we're fortunate) should not make us high-minded.

What does it mean to be high-minded? High-minded people think they're better than the less fortunate. If we are high-minded, stingy or greedy, God will not bless us mone-tarily because our hearts will not be able to handle it. The high-minded make the mistake of trusting their riches. Do not trust riches (1 Tim. 6:17); trust God, *Beloved, lean on Jesus.*

There is nothing that God will not give us. Jesus said, *"Fear not, little flock; for it is your Father's good pleasure to give you the kingdom" (Lu. 12:32).*

> *That they do good, that they be rich in good works,*
> *ready to distribute, willing to communicate.*
> *Laying up in store for themselves a good foun-*
> *dation against the time to come, that they may*
> *lay hold on eternal life. (1 Timothy 6:18-19)*

If we understand what God is saying to us through His Word, money will be viewed as an *opportunity* not an *obstacle.* Money is given the greatest value in the world, but the least in the kingdom of God.

Many churches cannot be trusted with money because their eyes are not single (Matt. 6:22). Only a single-eyed church warrants God's abundant blessings.

The world's view is, *"Money is power,"* therefore, making the person with money powerful. If this becomes our view, God may say: *"No wait a minute; let Me remove their money so they can get the proper perspective."*

If we believe money alone is powerful, we may pursue it and not pursue God. Make no mistake, *money can get us a lot of things, but it can't get everything.* Money can only buy things that are temporal, but don't settle for the *temporal* at the cost of the *eternal. The temporal is obtained by a **getting** mind-set; the eternal is acquired through a mind set on **giving**.*

Changing our view not only changes our lives, it changes the lives of others. Think about what we can contribute if we have millions of dollars. Think about others we can bless, neighborhoods we can enhance, jobs we can create, businesses we can help.

God wants to break the spirit of poverty off His people.

For they themselves show of us what manner
of entering in we had unto you, and how ye
turned to God from idols to serve the living
and true God. (1 Thessalonians 1:9)

Many people are just turning in circles going around and around. However, when we turn to God, we move forward. We turn to the true and living God; break the back of idols, mammon, and everything that personifies itself in the world.

The philosophy of the world says, *"Get all you can, can all you get, sit on the top and let the rest rot!"* When we turn to God, He liberates us; He teaches us *the more we give the more He gives to us.* Beloved, we can't beat God's giving no matter how we try.

Having the right view of our God makes all the difference. It causes us to give without limitations and it changes us while moving us from God's **good** to His **better** and eventually His very **best**.

God wants to bless us. He wants us to trust Him, not uncertain riches. He gives us all things to enjoy. Declare this now: *"I will not trust in riches; I will trust in my God. The result of my trust will bring me great gain, because I believe in the Great God!"*

CHAPTER FIVE
QUESTIONS FOR REFLECTION

How do you view God?

....

....

....

....

Your identity should be with

....

....

....

....

What has the least value in the kingdom of
God, yet the highest value in the world?

....

....

....

....

What does being single-eyed mean?

....

....

....

....

Name the first and eighth key of maturity:

....

....

....

....

Explain how your giving establishes your living.

....
....
....
....

According to the chapter explain the difference
between being godly and worldly.

....
....
....
....
....

How should you view your money?

....
....
....
....
....
....

6

LIVING IN GOD'S ECONOMY—PT. 1
A PROSPEROUS MINDSET

Every man according as he purposeth in his heart,
so let him give; not grudgingly, or of necessity: for
God loveth a cheerful giver. (2 Corinthians 9:7)

GIVING ESTABLISHES OUR LIVING in God's economy. The purpose of living is to glorify God through stewardship; this point can't be stated enough. I said the following already, but it bears reiterating. The Greek word for steward is oikonomos (Oikos means house and nomos means law), thus this word denotes manager of a household or estate; or house laws. This is essential because when we say God's economy, it comes from the word stewardship or steward.

The key point is to live off God's economy and not the world's. The Bible emphatically teaches us to live in the world and not be of the world. Once we receive Jesus as our Lord, we live by His kingdom principles. The first principle Jesus gave was *repent*.

The word repent is not a bad or negative word, it's a good term. However, the only time we hear the word repent is in church. The world deals with penance; but we are talking about repentance.

Let's look closer at the word repent. **Re** means to *come back to the place or come back again.* **Pent** is *the highest point, like a penthouse.* If a person makes it to the penthouse then they are at the top of that hotel. If a person commits a serious crime they are sent to the penitentiary. If you make it to the penitentiary you have made it to the "big house."

Because Adam and Eve fell, humanity fell. Therefore, Jesus came with the message of repentance; getting back to the place where God had us in the beginning.

The message of repentance deals with us changing our minds. *We change our minds by renewing our minds to the mind of Christ, and receiving His mind through His Word.*

The Word of God instructs us not to lean on our own understanding but in all of our ways acknowledge the Lord and He shall direct our path (Prov. 3:5-6). The Lord *directs, guides* and *leads* us. Wherever the Lord sends us, we are not going without Him. Therefore, it will do us well to live in God's economy.

THINKING FOR A CHANGE: A PROSPEROUS MINDSET

The mind of Christ is *the Word of God.* When Jesus came teaching repentance, He was saying change the way you think. ***Think for a change!*** In essence, the message of repentance is telling us to renew our minds to the mind of Christ. *The mind of Christ is a prosperous mindset.*

For if there be first a willing mind...
(2 Corinthians 8:12)

And not that only, but who was also chosen of the
churches to travel with us with this grace, which is
administered by us to the glory of the same Lord, and
declaration of your ready mind. (2 Corinthians 8:19)

The aforementioned scriptures admonish us to have both a willing and ready mind. This kind of mind leads to a prosperous mindset.

...Believe in the Lord your God, so shall
ye be established; believe his prophets, so
shall ye prosper. (2 Chronicles 20:20)

When we believe in God we are established and planted like a tree by the rivers of living water. Moreover, through God-given pastors teaching His Word, we experience prosperity. Prosperity carries the connotation of *"doing better."* God always wants us to do better.

The Lord wants us to progress from *faith to faith, strength to strength*, and *glory to glory*; that is doing better. He is always moving us forward. When we are not moving forward we are considered backsliders. We can move forward having a prosperous mindset. And a prosperous mindset begins with the right heart.

Every man according as he purposeth in his
heart, so let him give... (2 Corinthians 9:7)

A *purposeful* heart is a *prepared* heart. We prepare our hearts through the teaching of God's Word. It's impossible to have a prosperous mindset and a prosperous attitude without a prepared heart. When our hearts are established in the Word of God, our minds are renewed.

> *I beseech you therefore, brethren, by the mercies of*
> *God, that ye present your bodies a living sacrifice, holy,*
> *acceptable unto God, which is your reasonable service.*
> *And be not conformed to this world: but be ye trans-*
> *formed by the renewing of your mind... (Romans 12:1-2)*

Before receiving Christ into our lives we were a part of the world and we had the world's way of thinking. Our salvation should be evident by the way we think. Paul advised us not to be conformed to this world (pressed into this world's mold, image, likeness and thinking); rather to be transformed from this world. The word transformed is the Greek word *metamorphoo.* This is our English word metamorphosis.

In essence, like a caterpillar becomes a butterfly; and can never revert to a caterpillar, so we are to be transformed from this world to the kingdom of God. A caterpillar lives in the dirt, reduced to creeping and crawling. On the other hand, the butterfly takes to the air and is admired for its beauty. The life of the butterfly is what God wants for His people. A prosperous mindset causes us to fly high. It brings us from a life of dirt to connecting to the Divine.

> *I speak not by commandment, but by occasion*
> *of the forwardness of others, and to prove the*
> *sincerity of your love. (2 Corinthians 8:8)*

Giving is the proof of God's love operating in our lives. When we truly know God loves us we won't have a problem giving to others and giving to Him. A prosperous mindset certainly has

LIVING IN GOD'S ECONOMY PART ONE

its rewards. When we give it's given back to us a good measure, pressed down, shaken together and running over... (Lu. 6:38).

The book of Luke chapter 21 gives the account of a woman that gave her last bit of money to God. I'll admit when I was young in the faith this account bothered me. I wasn't bothered because I thought Jesus was cheating the woman; I just thought it unfair that she had given her absolute last. Later I discovered we serve a God who knows how to make our *last* become our *first*.

She had little, but much was given back to her in return. She proved the sincerity of her love for God and her prosperous mindset.

JESUS IS THE GIVER IN ME

When we receive Jesus Christ, the nature of God is in us. God's nature is a giving nature. The Jesus on the inside of us is the Giver in us, and He wants to be released.

I'm trying to get us into God's economy. The way we operate in God's economy is by becoming givers. This is how God funnels His *spiritual, material* and *financial* blessings in the earth. It cannot be under estimated when we give, it will come back to us measured out in great proportion (Lu. 6:38).

God gives seed to the sower and He multiplies the seed sown (2 Cor. 9:10). Another way of saying sower is giver. When we give to others with pure intentions God will always make us prosper.

It's like the farmer who says, *"Where is my harvest?"* And the ground replies, *"Where is the seed?"* There is no harvest if there is no planting. The farmer says, *"I'm looking for my harvest."* But the ground says, *"You haven't given me the seed."* When we give the ground a seed, it comes back good measure, and more than what we planted.

Every man according as he purposeth in his heart, so let him give; not grudgingly, or of necessity: (2 Corinthians 9:7)

When Jesus is in us we won't be able to help ourselves—we'll be compelled to give to others not just because there is a need. Paul told us not to be so "need" conscious that we give only out of necessity. Most people say, *"Well, she doesn't need anything. I don't see where he's lacking."* The person who says this lacks the understanding of *the principle of giving.*

We must determine how we are going to live. Are we going to live in God's economy or the economy of this world? If we live by the economy of this world, our lives will resemble a see-saw; up and down. However, God's economy fosters the concept; we must allow the Jesus in us to give through us. As this occurs, we'll see our lives go up and up and up.

David said I have never seen (in God's economy) the righteous forsaken and I've never seen His seed begging for bread (Ps. 37:25). We are talking about having a prosperous attitude, not an impoverished one. Do we live to **get** or do we live to **give**? All God is looking for is a channel, a funnel, like water coming through a pipe. If the pipe is blocked He can't get the water through. Albeit, if the passage is clear, water is distributed to others and the pipe (that's you and me) always gets wet. If we allow Jesus to give through us, our resources will never run dry.

The eyes of the Lord run to and fro throughout the whole earth to show Himself strong (2 Chr. 16:9). He looks for a channel and we determine our living by our giving. Jesus taught this in terms of stewardship. Everything we have belongs to God.

I recall a story I heard of a man dying and his preacher

came by to pay his last respects. The preacher encouraged him and said, *"Friend, you don't have to cry about dying; you're not going to go to Hell you're going to Heaven."* The man said, *"I'm not crying about where I'm going. I'm crying because I'm embarrassed to stand before God knowing I gave little to Him in this life."* The point is, our time is running out. Therefore, we need to allow Jesus to give through us so we need not be ashamed when we come face to face with our Lord.

JESUS: THE MAGNETISM OF OPTIMISM

There is a law I call and consider *"The Magnetism of Optimism."* The magnetism of optimism is Jesus. When Jesus is on the inside working on the outside, oh what a change He makes in our lives. The magnetism is God's divine ability; His grace. It's His grace and His favor to draw and to attract good people, things and opportunities.

Have you ever heard somebody say, *"Nothing good ever happens to me?" I've been waiting for Mr. or Ms. Right all these years."* The way we receive good people, things and opportunities is through the love of Jesus. When Jesus is on the inside of us it will show through small gestures such as a smile.

No one willingly decides to spend their time or their life around people with frowns. I have never seen anybody drawn to a person who doesn't smile every now and then. If you are one who has a grumpy countenance, look at yourself in the mirror and ask, *"Would I marry a person with that frown?"*

There is a magnetism that draws God's best when the joy of the Lord is our strength, so praise the Lord! There is a divine ability of grace and favor from God on every born-again believer's life. God's favor is on us; so use it. God placed His favor on you and me like He did with Joseph.

Joseph's brothers sold him into bondage. He could have walked around seeking pity, but he didn't. Joseph went from the pit to Potiphar's house. Potiphar liked Joseph and his wife wanted Joseph. Then due to events out of his control, Joseph was imprisoned. While there, the warden liked Joseph. Later Joseph was moved to the palace because God's favor was on him. Joseph found himself in a bad situation, but he never had a bad attitude.

Joseph had the Spirit of Christ operating in his life. This Spirit was the magnetism that brought about his optimism. He went from the pit—to Potiphar's slave—to prison, but the magnetism of Jesus landed him in the palace where he spent the remainder of his days in peace.

There is a magnetism of optimism and we must be optimistic. There is no in between. Either we are hot or cold. If we are lukewarm even God doesn't want us. God will regurgitate us (Rev. 3:16).

God wants us with optimism, but if we are pessimistic we are operating from the world's perspective. Sadly, there are too many negative Christians going to heaven with a bad attitude. Listen, positively or negatively, the choice is ours; sparingly or bountifully, the choice is ours.

A Father asked his son when he came home, *"Son, how did you do on your test today?"* The son said, *"Dad, I believe I failed."* The Father said, *"Son, I told you don't be negative; be optimistic. Be positive. Don't say you believe you failed! Do you hear me son?"* The son said, *"Yes dad, I do. I'm positive I failed."*

This is what God wants: even in a negative situation, be positive and have a prosperous mindset. The principle of giving establishes our living. Above all, remember we are living in God's economy.

CHAPTER SIX
QUESTIONS FOR REFLECTION

According to this chapter, explain what is meant by repentance.

....

....

....

....

....

....

What is meant by having the mind of
Christ? And how do you get it?

....

....

....

....

....

....

....

....

Are you living the life of a butterfly or
caterpillar? Explain your answer:

....

....

....

....

....

....

....

....

Are you operating in God's economy? If so, explain:

....
....
....
....
....
....
....

Explain the law of the magnetism of optimism:

....
....
....
....
....
....
....

7

LIVING IN GOD'S ECONOMY—PT. 2
THE FORWARDNESS OF YOUR MIND

For as touching the ministering to the saints, it is
superfluous for me to write to you: For I know the
forwardness of your mind, for which I boast of you to them
of Macedonia, that Achaia was ready a year ago; and your
zeal has provoked very many. (2 Corinthians 9:1-2)

THERE IS NOTHING LIKE living in the economy of God. God commanded the children of Israel to come out of Egypt (Ex. 3). Like Israel, we cannot come out unless we're willing to go up with Him. He took Peter, James and John up into a mountain with Him and they heard God speak (Matt. 17:1-5). His desire is to take us up just as He took them. In the book of Matthew chapter 5 we find the 12 disciples coming up to Jesus. While up, He taught them the *beatitudes* (which means let this be your attitude).

Attitude is so important because it deals with the mind and is a matter of the heart. It reveals what we meditate on and give ourselves to. God wants us to have a forward mind which denotes a positive and prosperous attitude. In 2nd Corinthians 9:2 we find this word forwardness conveying the *principle of giving* which establishes our living.

Giving establishes our living in God's economy. We cannot live in God's economy if we are not willing to give on a higher level. A lot of people don't live there (on a higher level) because they cannot give there. Living in God's economy means we must maintain a prosperous mindset and become sowers.

GOD GIVES SEED TO THE SOWER

> *But this I say, He which soweth sparingly shall reap also sparingly; and he which soweth bountifully shall reap also bountifully. (2 Corinthians 9:6)*

We must choose to sow either sparingly or bountifully. Some people don't sow at all and as the old adage goes, nothing from nothing leaves nothing. Thus, we got to sow something! God is not ever trying to rip us off; God is always trying to bless us exceedingly, abundantly, above all that we ask or think (Eph. 3:20). This fact is established in the text: *"He which soweth sparingly shall reap also sparingly and he which soweth bountifully shall reap also bountifully"* (2 Cor. 9:6).

Another timeless axiom is: *"You reap what you sow."* Fact is, sowing starts in the heart before it ever moves out of the hand. *"Every man according as he purposeth in his heart, so let him give..."* (2 Cor. 9:7). **A grateful heart establishes a giving hand.** A person will purpose in their heart to give when they are grateful for what they have been given. God has given something to all of us. When there is gratitude in the attitude, it lifts us to a higher altitude. It takes us where God wants us to live.

God wants us to live at a prosperous altitude. God is love (1 John 4:8) and love is conveyed through giving. God so loved, He gave His only begotten Son (John 3:16). When a person says, *"I love you,"* the corresponding action is giving. Love is the converse of lust. Lust is easily identified because it doesn't give it seeks to get or take. Remember, Jesus on the inside of us is the giver on the inside of us. To give means to sow and God gives seed to the sower.

It's imperative that we associate giving to sowing. A person may ask, *"Isn't sowing farmer lingo?"* Yes! We are to live by the same principles farmers live by. There is a direct correlation between our seed and our harvest. God gives us seed to meet our need. However, we must purpose in our hearts to be sowers of the seed God gives. *"Every man according as he purposeth in his heart, so let Him give; not grudgingly, or of necessity: for God loveth a cheerful giver" (2 Cor. 9:7).* If we are givers then we are sowers and sowers can count on God for seed.

> As it is written, He hath dispersed abroad;
> he hath given to the poor: his righteousness
> remaineth for ever. (2 Corinthians 9:9)

God desires the spirit of poverty to be broken off His people. However, if the preacher doesn't deliver God's prosperity message it won't happen. The Lord's message of prosperity is throughout the entire Bible. Yet many of God's preachers duck and dodge the Lord's message of prosperity because they fear people will say, *"You're trying to get in my pocket."* Listen,

God is not trying to get money from you; He's attempting to get money to you.

If the poor don't know the purpose of God's giving they'll remain poor. God gives seed to the sower. In essence, many are looking for God to extend His hand; while God is looking for us to be extensions of His hand. If we always have our hands out, we can't be helping hands to others. Therefore, we must see the seed as a means to an end. Our God-given seed is to meet our need and the needs of others. The poor never sow their seed. Instead of sowing, the poor usually eat their seed. The only way to move from the state of poverty to prosperity is through forwardness of your mind (giving).

When God gives you a dollar, holler, because you got something. God doesn't expect you to give the whole dollar. Nevertheless, some people won't even give God ten cents out of the dollar. They reason, *"Well, ten cents is nothing. I know God wants me to do more."* Beloved, it's not the amount; the blessing is in your obedience to give. What have you purposed in your heart? If a man won't give a little, he won't give much and if he won't give much, he will not receive much.

> *Now he that ministereth seed to the sower*
> *both minister bread for your food, and multi-*
> *ply your seed sown, and increase the fruits of*
> *your righteousness. (2 Corinthians 9:10)*

The aforementioned text reads: *He that ministers seed to the sower...* Now, I would like to bring attention to the suffix "er." The suffix "er" in just about any word establishes not just our confession but our profession. For instance, there are people who can dance, but they are not danc**er**s; sing but they are not sing**er**s; preach but they are not preach**er**s. So, the suffix "er" means we are professionals of what we are confessing. God wants us to become sow**er**s or giv**er**s; to become professionals at giving. This causes Him to use us as His channels of blessings while receiving His favor in the process.

God is going to take care of us. Even more, He wants us to be sowers. He brings multiplication into our lives, because He multiplies our seed sown. If there is no seed sown, there is no multiplying; there is no increase of the harvest. In fact, there is no harvest! Through the forwardness of our minds, He multiplies our seed sown and increases the fruits of our righteousness.

PROGRESSING WITH A FORWARD MIND

For I know the forwardness of your mind... (2 Corinthians 9:2)

Those who live in God's economy have developed a forward mind and are able to progress. Those with the forward mind place their faith in God and they expect to have God's ability released in their lives. Keep in mind; we can't release the ability of God if we are not living in the economy of God. Living in God's economy means we are equipped with His grace.

G God's
R Riches
A At
C Christ's
E Expense

Everything we receive from God comes through His love

and the grace of Jesus Christ. We can't exhaust the blessings of God. Consider the following verse of scripture:

> *And God is able to make all grace abound toward you;*
> *that ye, always having all sufficiency in all things,*
> *may abound to every good work. (2 Corinthians 9:8)*

The preceding scripture explains how God's economy functions. Listen again, *God is able*—the **might** of it, *to make all grace*—the **manner** of it, *abound toward you*—the **movement** of it, *that you always having all sufficiency in all things*—the **measure** of it, *may abound to every good work*—the **ministry** in it and of it.

The common working definition for faith in church circles is: *Forward action in trusting Him.* The way of God is always a forward movement.

> *And there was a famine in the land, beside the*
> *first famine that was in the days of Abraham. And*
> *Isaac went unto Abimelech king of the Philistines*
> *unto Gera. And the Lord appeared unto him, and*
> *said, Go not down into Egypt; dwell in the land*
> *which I shall tell thee of. (Genesis 26:1-2)*

The way of the forward mind is to progress; therefore, it is up, not down. Isaac and every child of God is instructed not to *go down into Egypt (Gen. 26:2)*. The church today is not to look at Egypt. We're not speaking of Egypt geographically, but spiritually. Egypt is a type of the world. In other words, God's instructions for His church today is, *"Don't go down in the world."* Even still, many of God's people do.

> *...Out of Egypt have I called my son. (Matthews 2:15)*

God is still calling His sons and daughters out of the world. He wants us out of the world's debt and death grip. The world's system of debt can place such a burden on God's people that at times it feels like death. In fact, The word mortgage is derived from a French law term used by English lawyers in the middle ages meaning "death pledge," and refers to the pledge ending (dying) when either the obligation is fulfilled or the property is taken through foreclosure. I'm not stating mortgages are evil; God wants us to own property. However, the term mortgage serves as a reminder, debt can correlate with death.

Too much accumulated debt pulls people down. God wants His people in place to be the lenders and not always the borrowers (Prov. 22:7). I am talking about a forward mind. The mindset is connected to the concept and the concept is prosperity. One particular African tribe doesn't recognize the term prosperous. It's not incorporated in their vocabulary. Instead, they use the phrase *"To do better."* Prosperity is not only in the area of money, prosperity simply means to do better; to progress.

Whether we are single or married, in an apartment or house, unemployed or employed, whatever our present condition, we should always want to do better. We should always seek ways to move forward. If we are moving backwards it's called backsliding.

Everyone should have a desire to do better. You may say, *"I already have a good marriage,"* it can get better. If we are not progressing we are digressing. Our lives ought to be getting better. The Lord gets sweeter and sweeter as the days go by and He wants us to progress as well.

> *...Go not down into Egypt; dwell in the land which*
> *I shall tell thee of: Sojourn in this land, and I will*

*be with thee, and will bless thee; for unto thee,
and unto thy seed, I will give all these countries,
and I will perform the oath which I sware unto
Abraham thy father; And I will make thy seed to
multiply as the stars of heaven..." (Genesis 26:2-4)*

Genesis chapter 26 verse 12 records: *"Then Isaac sowed in
that land..."* In a land of famine where it appeared nothing was
happening, Isaac sowed and received. The news anchors and
analysts report how the economy is devastated at both micro
and macro levels. However, there's another economy; God's
economy.

The kingdom of heaven is not motivated by what's happening in the economy of this world. Beloved, *"My God shall
supply all of your need..." (Phil. 4:19)*. God is able to make a
crooked thing straight. What's impossible with man is not
impossible with God.

*Then Isaac sowed in that land, and received
in the same year an hundredfold: and the
Lord blessed him. (Genesis 26:12)*

Don't look at man; look at God. Isaac looked at God, he
heard what God was saying and did not allow the economy
of that day to prohibit his giving. He knew his blessing was
coming from the Lord. It wasn't predicated upon the economy;
it was determined by the forwardness of his mind.

*And the man waxed great, and went forward, and
grew until he became very great. (Genesis 26:13)*

He had a mindset that was connected to the concept *"To
do better."* Where is your mindset? If your mind is not set, it
fluctuates up and down like the Dow Jones of this economy.

This was not the case with Isaac. He grew, there was progression. Prosperity is progression. Isaac had to grow, he had to progress. He grew until he became very great.

> *For he had possession of flocks, and possession of herds, and great store of servants: and the Philistines envied him. (Genesis 26:14)*

The Philistines looked at Isaac and wondered, *"How can this guy be so prosperous during hard times?"* Today, the Lord wants His church to make the world wonder *"How can they accomplish this? How can they afford that?"* We are God's people. God hasn't called us to dwell in Egypt; He called us out of Egypt (Matt. 2:15). We may be in the world but we are not of the world (John 15:19). *We must **grow up** before we **go out; look up** before we **look out;** only then can we **move forward.***

GOD IS MOVING US FORWARD

God sent Moses to bring His people out of bondage. He sends pastors today with that same purpose. Pastors are called by God to move the people forward.

> *And I will give you pastors according to mine heart, which shall feed you with knowledge and understanding. And it shall come to pass, when ye be multiplied and increased in the land, in those days, saith the Lord... (Jeremiah 3:15-16)*

God gives pastors so the people may *increase* and *multiply.* The spirit of the Lord is upon pastors and they are anointed to preach the gospel to the poor (Lu. 4:18). Pastors deliver God's Word to move people forward. There is a burden removing yoke destroying power of God resting upon His Word. If you believe and receive God's Word, He will change the dynamics in your life and in your family.

God wants us to be like trees planted by the rivers of living waters, and whatever we do shall prosper (Ps. 1:3). God is going to cause us to be *the head* and not *the tail, above only* and not *beneath* (Deut. 28:13). God is moving us above only. It doesn't matter if the economy is bad, whether your family is poor, God can break poverty with a forward mindset. Confess now, *"I'm moving forward."*

Don't settle for mediocrity. God wants us to do more. He wants us to let Him show His strength and authority. The eyes of the Lord run throughout the whole earth (2 Chron. 16:9). God doesn't want us going back into Egypt. God's calling us out. For this reason, He wrote a whole book called Exodus—*so make your Exit!*

> *And Moses said unto the people, Fear ye not, stand still, and see the salvation of the Lord, which he will shew to you to day: for the Egyptians whom ye have seen to day, ye shall see them again no more for ever. (Exodus 14:13)*

God released the cohesiveness of the water in the Red Sea. Sure, the water swallowed the Egyptians, but more importantly, God closed the door. The Lord was eliminating the opportunity for His people to return to their negative ways. *No more going back! The way for us today, is forward.*

Four lepers said, *"Why sit we here until we die"* (2 Ki. 7:3). In essence, they said, *"Let us rise and go forward."* They decided to travel to the enemy's camp and God caused the enemy to flee because they heard a sound from heaven. The four lepers had a forward mindset and God gave them the spoils of the enemy because of it.

Faith is forward action in trusting Him. God will make a way where there is no way, if we move forward. Paul said, *"I know the forwardness of your mind" (2 Cor. 9:2)*. Beloved, let there be gratitude in your attitude, just praise the Lord for His goodness and He'll lift you up.

The Lord wants us to see, take and keep His blessings. He wants us to experience *more than enough*, not *just enough*. No more just having enough to take care of you and your family. No, it's time to move forward in God's abundance. Sure, people will envy you and ask, *"How did you do it?"* Just smile and reply, *"I'm living in God's economy."*

CHAPTER SEVEN
QUESTIONS FOR REFLECTION

According to this chapter, what two things are
needed in order to live in God's economy?

1. ....

2. ....

Are you grateful? If so, list some of the
things for which you are grateful.

....

....

....

....

....

....

....

Explain the difference between love and lust.

....

....

....

....

....

....

God gives seed to sowers. Explain the purpose of the seed:

....

....

....

....

....

....

Grace is:

G ....

R ....

A ....

C ....

E ....

How can having a forward mind-set better your life?

....

....

....

....

....

....

....

....

....

THE PATTERN OF RECEIVING

{SECTION III}

8

THE PATTERN OF RECEIVING

But this I say, He which soweth sparingly shall reap also sparingly; and he which soweth bountifully shall reap also bountifully. Every man according as he purposeth in his heart, so let him give; not grudgingly, or of necessity: for God loveth a cheerful giver. And God is able to make all grace abound toward you; that ye, always having all sufficiency in all things, may abound to every good work. 2 Corinthians 9:6-8

GOD WANTS US TO RECEIVE. Therefore, I want to discuss the pattern of receiving which modifies our lifestyle and elevates our living conditions. How we live, where we live and what we receive is a result of our thinking. In other words, *if we want to change the outcome of our living, we must change the income of our thinking*. Our thinking changes as our heart is changed.

It is the Lord who gives us a changed heart. Although God changes our hearts, we must change our minds. Therefore, if we are going to change the outcome of our living, we must change the income of our thinking about giving.

The world's mantra is get, get, get—that's greedy! Greed teaches *get all you can; can all you got; sit on the top and let the rest rot.* Nevertheless, through God our hearts and minds are changed, and we become givers, not takers in life.

By no means am I criticizing or condemning anyone in terms of being poor or poverty-stricken, but God does not want His children poor anymore. God wants you to have a prosperous mindset and determine in your heart, *"I am a cheerful giver (2 Cor. 9:7)."*

GIVING: RELEASE GOD'S ABILITY

> *And God is able to make all grace abound toward you;*
> *that ye, always having all sufficiency in all things,*
> *may abound to every good work: 2 Corinthians 9:8*

Extend me the liberty of repeating; you hold the key to release God's ability, grace, and favor upon your situation. According to the previous scripture God is able and this is the *might* of it. To make all grace is the *manner* of it. Abound towards you, the *motion* and the *movement* of it. That you always having all sufficiency in all things is the *measure* of it. Nothing is lacking that you may abound to every good work is the *ministry* of it.

God's Word conveys we attack our lack by releasing His ability. God gives us a seed to attack our lack. However, only through the pattern of receiving do we get in on what God is doing. The pattern of receiving is *giving what you need* and *want to receive*!

> *Now he that ministereth seed to the sower*
> *both minister bread for your food, and multi-*
> *ply your seed sown, and increase the fruits of*
> *your righteousness. 2 Corinthians 9:10*

Too often the *pattern* of receiving is interrupted by the *problem* of receiving. The problem is the poor eat the seed God gives rather than sowing it. Jesus said the Spirit of the Lord is upon me, and He has anointed me to preach the gospel to the poor (Luke 4:18). What is the Gospel? It is the good news. Good news to a poor man is, *"You are not going to be poor anymore and your broke days are over."*

Seed is only considered seed because it's not enough to meet the need. A farmer's seed is planted to produce the harvest; it's not the harvest. God gives seed to plant by faith and we're able to watch Him meet our need. God is trying to get us to operate from His economy; therefore, we must change the income of our thinking by becoming givers. Our seed is the key that releases God's ability to change the outcome of our living.

I recall the initial stages of the church I pastor and how I released God's ability in my life and ministry.

We started with 14 members. They wanted to contribute financially toward starting the church. I was thankful, but would not allow them to do so. I used my own paycheck toward the opening of the church. I put my faith and money where my mouth was. I remember thinking; this will be the fastest church in and out of business, because if God wasn't in it, I wasn't doing it.

The members said, *"We have to put up a sign so people will know this is a church?"* I said, *"No sign!"* My resolve was, *"If God does not meet the need in 30 days; we will close on day 31."* I didn't have to pastor a church; I was content simply going to church.

Faith is released by *saying, doing* or *giving* something. By giving my own paycheck I released the ability of God to get in on the project and direct it toward success.

There was a man who owned a carpet business. On the Saturday before our first Sunday service, God moved on his heart to bless us. I didn't even know the man and he put carpet in our first location. My pastor came and said, *"Brother Nate, you are going to need a pulpit."* I responded, *"All I have is my paycheck. I don't have enough to pay for a pulpit."* He continued, *"I'm a carpenter and I'm going to build you a pulpit."* He built my first pulpit within 3 hours. The church also received movie theater chairs from a pastor in Kempner, Texas. Everything occurred as the scripture reads, *the lines were falling in pleasant places* (Ps. 16:6).

We started the church with one paycheck and less than 20 members, but our faith was in the living God and now we serve over 3,000 members weekly. I believed then and still today God wants us to live off His economy. He wants us blessed coming in and going out; in the city and in the field.

I remember preachers would ask me, *"Why start a church in a little city like Copperas Cove?"* They continued, *"You've come all the way from Philadelphia by way of California to begin a work in Copperas Cove!"* Listen, Copperas Cove is where God assigned us; therefore, it's where God will bless us. As long as you're in the will of God, He will bless you *exceeding, abundantly above all that you can ask and even think (Eph. 3:20).*

When we allow God's ability to come forth through our giving, He is able to make all grace abound toward us (2 Cor. 9:8). God loves a cheerful giver and the moment you give you release God's ability upon your life.

GIVE AND IT SHALL BE GIVEN

There is a word called anti-metronomos and it deals with the principle, give and it shall be given back to you. Let's break down the word anti-metronomos. In the original Greek language *anti* means *opposite to, from or against*; **metro** is *measure* and **nomos** means *law*. This is the law of giving and receiving.

The *pattern of receiving* is giving what you need or want to receive. When you do, it shall be given back to you. Some may say, *"I don't have any money but I can give in another way."* However, if you're looking to get money you have to give money. According to the law of anti-metronomos, "it" comes back and "it" represents whatever you give.

God operates in a supernatural way. However, He wants to establish us as *cheerful* givers. The same way God supernaturally opened the Red Sea, He will open doors of opportunity for His people. Jesus said if you give it, it will be given back to you. A *good measure, pressed down, shaken together* and *running over* shall men give into your bosom. The same measure you give, it will be measured to you again (Lu. 6:38). He says if a person does it stingily, it comes back stingily; if you give bountifully it returns that way.

God will give you a new heart but you must change your mind. You've got to **think for a change**. Stop thinking the old way. I know everything was tight or not right in the world, but you cannot discount God's law of giving. In Genesis 13, we are given examples through Abraham and Lot. Through these men I discovered a principle of life which I call, ***"Ordained to be With."***

> *And he ordained twelve, that they*
> *should be with him... (Mark 3:14)*

Lot was prosperous because he was with Abraham. When Lot separated from Abraham he lost everything. However, Lot recovered everything when he reconnected with Abraham (Gen. 14:12-16).

Some people prosper with their leader and then they leave and lose what they have, because they were ordained to be with their leader.

God gave Abraham a promise. Lot prospered because he was with Abraham (Gen. 13:1-6). The Bible then records: *"And there was strife between the herdmen of Abram's cattle and the herdmen of Lot's cattle..." (v. 7).*

Then Abraham said to Lot this strife between us is not right because we are family. He further expressed:

> *Is not the whole land before you? Separate yourself,*
> *I beg of you, from me. If you take the left hand,*
> *then I will go to the right; or if you choose the right*
> *hand, then I will go to the left. (Genesis 13:9 AMP)*

Lot, thinking only of himself, saw the grass was greener on the other side.

> *And Lot looked and saw that everywhere the*
> *Jordan Valley was well watered. Before the Lord*
> *destroyed Sodom and Gomorrah, [it was all] like*
> *the garden of the Lord... (Genesis 13:10 AMP)*

Lot should have offered Abraham the well watered land because God made the promise to Abraham. Instead he chose selfishly and paid dearly as a result. Lot chose the land of the Jordan Valley and pitched his tent toward Sodom.

> *But the men of Sodom were wicked and exceedingly*
> *great sinners against the Lord. (Genesis 13:13 AMP)*

After Lot separated from his uncle, the Lord said to Abraham:

*...Lift up now your eyes and look from the
place where you are, northward and southward
and eastward and westward; For all the land
which you see I will give to you and to your
posterity forever. (Genesis 13:14-15 AMP)*

Lot was seeking to take and never give. Consequently, he lost it all because he never understood how he got it. This brings to mind a principle mentioned earlier: "See, take and keep."

- **See**—Some people see it, but never take it.

- **Take**—Some people take it, but never keep it.

- **Keep**—God wants us to keep what He has given us.

If we do not understand how we received what we have, we will not be able to keep it. Keeping what we have means operating from the pattern of receiving. The pattern of receiving functions on the premise, give and it shall be given back to you.

Abraham operated in the pattern of receiving and attacked his lack by giving—tithes of all. He did not *pay* tithes he *gave* tithes of all he received (Gen. 14:20). And when Abraham was propositioned by the king of Sodom, he responded:

*...I have lift up mine hand unto the LORD, the most
high God, the possessor of heaven and earth, That I will
not take from a thread even to a shoelatchet, and that I
will not take anything that is thine, lest thou shouldest
say, I have made Abram rich. (Genesis 14:22-23)*

Abraham was determined not to allow anybody to take the glory from God. God is the One who blesses us coming in and going out. Abraham told the king of Sodom, *"I am not going to take even a shoe latch from you and have you saying, 'I am the one that made Abraham rich.'"* God makes a way where there is no way and no one deserves or gets His glory. If God be for us who and what can be against us and succeed?

Lot had a heart of greed and never looked to give God anything. As a result he suffered tremendous loss. On the contrary, Abraham operated through the *pattern of receiving.* He did not withhold anything from the Lord and reaped a bountiful harvest in return.

THE PATTERN IS PROSPEROUS

When I first got saved and understood God's command concerning giving I became a tither. The moment I became a tither I opened the door to the *pattern of receiving.* It was so exciting to trust God in the area of my giving. As I began my Christian walk, I learned, I couldn't beat God's giving no matter how I tried. The more I gave the more He gave to me.

Allow me to share a time when God met my family's need. When I moved my family to the Fort Hood, Texas area I met with a rental person to acquire a place to live. At the time, I was a Private in the military. The rental guy showed me one place after another that he felt a Private in the Army could afford. I was not pleased with any of the rentals he offered.

Finally I requested, *"Show me the best rental homes. Let's start at the top and work our way down."* He replied, *"Majors and Captains reside in these expensive homes and some of them can't afford it and you're only a Private!"*

I counter replied, *"Don't worry about my position—show*

me the best!" When we drove to the next home, I said, *"This could be the place."* Again, he retorted, *"You're not going to be able to afford it!"* We walked into that home; I removed my hat, bowed my head and prayed. God spoke to me and said, *"This is it!"* *"This is where I want you to live."*

After praying, I told the realtor, *"God just spoke to me."* I informed him that we would take the place and I gave him 6 months' rent in advance. I asked him to handle getting my water and lights on and gave him the money. He agreed to do it and we never fell behind on our rent or utility payments because God supplies.

No matter if you are considered the least in your family; God will lift you from the gutter most to the uttermost. We have to change our thinking. We can't beat God giving. God wants to establish us as *cheerful* givers so we can get in the *pattern of receiving.* And this pattern is prosperous.

David understood this pattern because he was a poor man himself. David said, *"I have been young, and now am old; yet have I not seen the righteous forsaken, nor his seed begging bread"* (Ps. 37:25).

Beloved whatever you want start by giving it. Operate by faith in the *pattern of receiving.* Attack your lack by giving. By doing this, God will make all grace abound towards you. W. E. Vines Dictionary of Old and New Testament Words translates the word abound as *perisseia.* Perisseia carries the meaning of an *exceeding measure and abundance.* Grace is God's unmerited favor in abundance.

Money is a grace also. God's grace empowers us to accomplish what we need. Therefore, the Lord will use money to provide for the needs of His people. God will make money come to us. Like a magnetic pull, no matter where we run, money is coming to us. We turn this way and money is coming. If we turn in the other direction, money is coming.

> Sojourn in this land, and I will be with thee, and will
> bless thee; for unto thee, and unto thy seed, I will give
> all these countries, and I will perform the oath which
> I sware unto Abraham thy father. (Genesis 26:3)

We hold the key to releasing God's prosperity. Because of some people's hesitation to function in the *pattern of receiving,* God is unable to bless them. They fail to understand the pattern is prosperous.

Isaac knew firsthand the pinch of poverty. He dwelt in a barren land and lack engulfed the economy of the entire nation. In the midst of scarcity, Isaac fought back by sowing a seed. In essence, he operated in the *pattern of receiving "And received in the same year a hundredfold: and the LORD blessed him"* (Genesis 26:12).

People often make decisions on where to live or work based on the economy. Upon arrival many of these people discover unfavorable conditions. When things fail to pan out; these same people look elsewhere. The point is; don't move without receiving confirmation from God.

Listen for the voice of God. He will tell you what land and ministry to sow into. God's economy is not based upon **the geography of the land**. God's economy is revealed by **the Sovereignty of His hand**. Isaac sowed during the time of famine and in the same year he received a hundred-fold return.

> And the man waxed great, and went forward,
> and grew until he became very great: For he had
> possession of flocks, and possession of herds,

and great store of servants, and the Philistines
envied him. (Genesis 26:13-14)

Everybody envied Isaac because it appeared he had the Midas touch. The *pattern of receiving* brought him prosperity. The Lord has given the *pattern of receiving*, which is to attack our lack by giving what we need and want to receive.

The following scripture conveys the very heart of God concerning the *pattern of receiving*.

> *Give away your life; you'll find life given back, but*
> *not merely given back—given back with bonus*
> *and blessing. Giving, not getting, is the way.*
> *Generosity begets generosity. (Luke 6:38 MSG)*

If you haven't experienced the power of the *pattern of receiving* in your life, begin today. And discover how giving activates God's ability. Remember, when you give generously it shall be given back because the pattern is prosperous.

CHAPTER EIGHT
QUESTIONS FOR REFLECTION

How do you attack your lack?

....

....

....

How are you to operate the pattern of receiving?

....

....

....

How are you to release your faith?

....

....

....

According to the chapter, explain anti-metronomos:

....

....

....

Explain the principle Ordained to be With:

....

....

....

....

How do you get out of a personal famine?

....

....

....

....

9

FORGIVENESS KEEPS THE HEART BELIEVING

And when ye stand praying, forgive, if ye have ought against any: that your Father also which is in heaven may forgive you your trespasses. But if ye do not forgive, neither will your Father which is in heaven forgive your trespasses. (Mark 11:25-26)

GOD HAS A GIVING NATURE. He gives us His life, light and love. Albeit, before we can possess a giving nature we have to practice forgiveness. *Forgiveness keeps the heart believing.* In Jesus' dying words on the cross, He said, *"Father forgive them..." (Luke 23:34)*. Forgiving is a heart issue. God wants us to have a heart that forgives. We are His people, and we need His believing heart.

Naturally, the **physical heart beats** while the **spiritual heart believes**. If the physical heart stops beating, we die. If the spiritual heart stops believing, we become dead men walking. We are dead, neutered, impotent, void and powerless. At that point we become unbelieving believers.

FORGIVENESS: THE DEFENSE FOR THE OFFENSE

Forgiveness is the defense for any offense that comes our way. We are Believers because we trust Jesus Christ is Lord. He can shield and shape us through any offense. I consider a failure to forgive a spiritual heart attack. Fact is; offenses are inevitable. People will offend us and we will offend others. The important thing is to forgive to keep our hearts believing. God needs our hearts believing in order to operate in the *pattern of receiving.*

I commonly teach four laws of faith that every Believer must operate from to walk according to God's will. These laws keep our hearts trusting in the living God.

> *1. The **Person** of Faith—God is the object of our faith. He is the origin of faith. Jesus said, "...Have faith in God" (Mark 11:22).*

> *2. The **Principle** of Faith—A principle is a fixed law of operation that leaves no room for negotiation, debate, or discussion. This principle is the law of confession. Jesus said, "...For verily I say unto you Whosoever shall say (the law of confession is say what the word says) unto this mountain, be thou removed, and be thou cast into the sea; and shall not doubt in his heart, but shall believe that those things which he saith shall come to pass; he shall have whatsoever he saith" (Mark 11:23 parenthesis added). Your confession is your possession!*

> *3. The **Prayer** of Faith—The law of prayer is effective when we believe we receive what we pray for when we pray. Jesus said, "...What things so ever ye*

> *desire, when ye pray, believe that ye receive them, and ye shall have them"* (Mark 11:24).

4. *The* **Problem** *of Faith—The problem of faith is un-forgiveness. Jesus said, "...And when ye stand praying, forgive, if ye have ought against any: that your Father also which is in heaven may forgive you your trespasses"* (Mark 11:25). *Forgiveness keeps the heart believing and prepares it for receiving.*

We must understand the power and profundity of forgiveness. Forgiveness enables us to help ourselves. Jesus instructed His disciples to pray, *"...Give us day by day our daily bread. And forgive us our sins; for we also forgive every one..."* (Lu. 11:3-4).

Many times, we fail to forgive someone because we feel they do not deserve to be forgiven. However, it is imperative we understand ***forgiveness is the defense that helps us overcome the offense***.

Forgiveness is not so much for the offender's benefit as it is for ours. An offense not forgiven goes underneath the skin. It eats away at our hearts and before you know it, our heart is bleeding.

A bleeding heart creates a dead heart. A believing heart remains alive and strong. When something happens to you, it is the enemy's plot, ploy and plan to harden your heart.

A bleeding heart stems from hurts. Hurts caused by offenses stay in you causing you to become a hardhearted person. Within a few hours of death, a person's entire body turns cold. Today there are people walking around cold and stiff. David tells us, *"Enter into his gates with thanksgiving, and into his courts with praise... (Ps. 100:4)."* Un-forgiveness causes rigor mortis and people are unable to lift their hands to praise their God. Without forgiveness operating in our lives, it becomes hard to believe and obey God.

Forgiveness is the defense which keeps us in the joy of the Lord. Some people have allowed the offenses of others to steal their joy. When someone offends you just smile knowing the Lord defends the innocent. If you're happy; notify your face. In other words, get a facelift! Don't walk around all day with a somber look. The devil wants to pull your countenance *down to a frown*. He wants to make you doubt because doubting leads to fear and unbelief.

An unbelieving heart is a bleeding heart. A bleeding heart makes life dim, while a believing heart keeps your countenance bright. ***The brighter your outlook; the brighter your outcome***, therefore, you can overcome every offense the adversary brings your way.

OVERCOME THE OFFENSE

> *And if he trespass against thee seven times in a*
> *day, and seven times in a day turn again to thee,*
> *saying, I repent; thou shalt forgive him. (Luke 17:4)*

Peter asked the Lord a question concerning forgiveness. He wanted to know how many times in a day should he forgive a person. Peter enquired if he should forgive 7 times in a day. Jesus' response was to forgive 70 times 7 (Matt. 18:21-22). Keep in mind forgiving 70 times 7 was ascribed for a day not a year. That is 490 times! If you can forgive somebody 490 times in one day, one more time is not going to hurt.

The Lord is teaching us to overcome offenses. If we bear un-forgiveness, we prohibit God's blessings from reaching us. Listen, we all get hurt; however, the ability to overcome the offense allows healing to manifest.

If we do not forgive, we create a roadblock. Many times God has answered our prayers, but they have been hindered because there is a roadblock of un-forgiveness.

Picture this. You have ordered some furniture and have been waiting all morning for the delivery. Finally, the delivery man calls and tells you that he has your furniture, but there is a roadblock hindering him from getting to your house. He further explains as soon as the roadblock is removed he will deliver your furniture.

For some of us, it's not that our prayers have not been heard, God is unable to deliver answers due to the roadblock. The hindrance of un-forgiveness needs to be removed and it is removed when we forgive others offences toward us.

Jesus said, *"It is impossible but that offences will come..."* (Lu. 17:1). In the original Greek, the word offence is translated as *scandalizo*. This is where we get our English word scandalized. The word *scandalizo* carries the meaning of a *satanic snare or trap; to cause or give someone an occasion to fail or fall.*

In 2 Corinthians 2:11 the Bible says, *"...For we are not ignorant of his devices."* The word device is the Greek word *noema*. The noema of Satan is his **plot, ploy,** and **plan**. The devil plans for us to fail. His plot and ploy occurs through the offense of others. Therefore, we must foil the noema of Satan by getting over the offense through forgiveness.

> *And (Jesus) said to His disciples, Temptations (snares, traps set to entice to sin) are sure to come, but woe to him by or through whom they come! (Luke 17:1 AMP)*

When someone does something wrong to you or something bad happens and you are affected negatively, this is *scandalizo*. It causes you to *distrust*, *disbelieve* and *desert* your faith.

Our hearts should be full of faith and forgiveness. A forgiving heart is needed everywhere, in any occasion and with everyone. We can lead reclusive lives and still encounter offenses. Sometimes the people closest to us hurt us the most. The inability to overcome the offenses can leave us with broken, bleeding hearts.

Eventually, someone will break your heart. Your feelings will get hurt. Sooner or later, someone will come along and say or act unpleasantly. When this happens resist the temptation to knock them out. We won't get the victory through violence. The victory is obtained through temperance and temperance allows forgiveness.

Many never experience God's *pattern of receiving* because they take matters into their own hands rather than leaving them in the trustworthy hands of God. To overcome offenses, we have to **face it**, **trace it**, **erase it** and then **replace it**. We may face the offense or even trace it, but if we fail to erase it through forgiveness, we'll become a time-bomb.

People who fail to function in God's forgiveness walk with a **tick—tock—tick—tock** and eventually someone *ticks them off.* Suddenly, they explode! *The truth of the matter is hurt people, hurt people.* God doesn't want us hurt; He wants us healed so we can experience His pattern of receiving.

> *For whatsoever is born of God overcometh the*
> *world: and this is the victory that overcom-*
> *eth the world, even our faith.* (1 John 5:4)

We can overcome any offense with faith in God. Through faith we trust God's way is better than our own. God's way is forgiveness. Satan wants a toehold, then a foothold and ultimately a stronghold. He gains a stronghold when we fail to forgive. However, his plan is thwarted when we give him no place (Eph. 4:27). Forgiveness gives him no place, makes us overcomers and removes the roadblock for God's blessings.

There are three components to overcome offenses:

First, *confront it*—acknowledge the offense. Many people do not want to confront the offense. If somebody offends you, do not dismiss it saying, *"I am not going to let that bother me."* It is going to bother you. Confront it and forgive that person.

We should confront the issue. Confronting it means taking it to the Lord and talking to Him about it. Why talk to everybody else about your problem or what somebody else has done to you? They cannot do anything about it. Simply confront it by acknowledging what happened and forgive.

Second, *confess it*—announce it. In other words announce your forgiveness when you have been hurt or wronged. Just confess it to God. That is what Jesus did. They crucified Him and He said, *"Father forgive them..."* (Lu. 23:34).

Third, *commit it*—appeal to God the righteous judge. To commit it is to trust the Lord. God sees what happens and will handle the offense in His timing, His way. Peter reveals the way to handle the offenses of others, *"Who, when he was reviled, reviled not again; when he suffered, he threatened not. but committed himself to him that judgeth righteously"* (1 Pet. 2:23).

We must learn how to overcome every offense so we don't hinder the blessings of God in our lives. The Lord's *pattern of receiving* is released when we forgive. The Lord is real; He will return and ultimately repay anyone who offends and has not sought His forgiveness.

GOD WILL JUDGE THE OFFENDER

> But whoso shall offend one of these little ones which believe in me, it were better for him that a millstone were hanged about his neck, and that he were drowned in the depth of the sea. (Matthew 18:6)

The authorities such as parents, pastors and police officers should be trusted with the lives of the innocent. However, some people in authority have abused their power by scandalizing those who trust them. When offenders scandalize without regard distrust is spawn. Those who naturally believe no longer believe. When this happens God must judge the matter.

> Woe unto the world because of offences! for it must needs be that offences come; but woe to that man by whom the offence cometh! (Matthew 18:7)

The word woe carries with it an automatic attachment of punishment. In other words, you reap what you sow. Every day we are either sowing to the spirit, or to the flesh.

When a person mistreats you there's no need for reprisal *"...vengeance is mine; I will repay, saith the Lord"* (Rom. 12:19). You don't have to say to the offender, *"I'm going to get you back."* The principle: an eye for an eye, tooth for a tooth, never stops with eyes and teeth.

When an unforgiving person is wronged, an eye for an eye is not enough. They want the eye, arm, and leg. When someone wrongs you revenge is never the answer. Revenge is wrong and two wrongs never make it right. The devil plans to instill a bleeding heart within us, but God wants to keep our hearts believing.

There's an old saying, *"Misery loves company."* We are going to be scandalized but woe to the one who brings it. Whoever scandalizes others without remorse will be miserable. God is beckoning us to help and not hurt ourselves. He has given us the power of forgiveness to serve as a defense overcoming any offense we experience.

Some people are carrying old offenses. They hold on to things the Lord desires they let go. In order to move toward our future we must let go of transgressions that took place in the past. The level of a man's maturity is his ability to let go and go on in life.

Forgiveness keeps the heart believing, but un-forgiveness produces a bleeding and hard heart. If unforgiven offenses are allowed to fester and grow they produce anger and malice.

> *Ye have heard that it was said of them of old time,*
> *Thou shalt not kill; and whosoever shall kill shall be*
> *in danger of the judgment: But I say unto you, That*
> *whosoever is angry with his brother without a cause*
> *shall be in danger of the judgment... (Matthew 5:21-22)*

There are two concepts concerning anger that we must learn.

    1. **Thermal**—*is an internal attitude of anger.*
    2. **Orge**—*is an external action of violence.*

If we do not forgive, the offense will continue to grow. It just keeps swelling, boiling, until there is an eruption. An internal attitude of anger is like a volcanic eruption. It's like hot water. Hot water is 211°, but one more degree, at 212°, it is

boiling. It is no longer called hot water. It's boiling, tick—tock—
tick—tock, and then suddenly there's an external explosion.

> Let all bitterness, and wrath, and anger, and clamour,
> and evil speaking, be put away from you, with all
> malice: And be ye kind one to another, tenderhearted,
> forgiving one another, even as God for Christ's
> sake hath forgiven you. (Ephesians 4:31-32)

Beloved, forgiveness removes the roadblock that keeps
us from the *pattern of receiving*. There's absolutely no need to
defend yourself or seek payback for wrong deeds. Only God
resides as the righteous Judge, so let Him decide who deserves
what.

Let's practice the art of forgiving. Forgiveness keeps our
heart believing and a believing heart sets the stage for God's
blessings.

CHAPTER NINE
QUESTIONS FOR REFLECTION

How can you become an unbelieving believer?

....

....

....

....

Describe the difference between a believing
heart and a bleeding heart.

....

....

....

....

Briefly explain the Four Laws of Faith:

....

....

....

....

....

....

Is there an offence you are currently
struggling with? If so, what is it?

....

....

....

....

....

....

What are the four steps to recovering from any offence?

    1...

    2...

    3...

    4...

What are three components to overcome offenses? Explain them:

....

....

....

....

....

....

....

10

HARVEST GUARANTEED

Let him that is taught in the word communicate unto
him that teacheth in all good things. (Galatians 6:6)

JESUS INSTRUCTED US TO PRAY God's kingdom come and for His will to be done in our lives. His instructions correlate with God's *pattern of receiving*. Whether positive or negative, God has established our harvest is guaranteed. However, the preparatory action to our harvest is that we communicate.

Communicate is an interesting word in that it could convey a myriad of messages. This word *communicate* could be used to express the common joy two or more people share. It's often utilized as a means to disseminate information to others. However, in the aforementioned scripture Paul used the term *communicate* to illustrate exchange; it deals with giving and receiving.

In our economy we are encouraged to consume every-thing, but in order to receive anything we must communicate. Everywhere we go we owe. Whether we go to see a movie, or dine in a restaurant, we have to communicate.

To communicate is a principle instated by God. As we operate according to this principle we will experience a guaranteed harvest in our lives.

GOD'S BLESSING GUARANTEES HIS HARVEST

And let us not be weary in well doing: for in due season we shall reap, if we faint not. (Galatians 6:9)

God has established in His Word the harvest is guaranteed in due season if we faint not. Our harvest will be positive or negative depending on what we sow. The Lord's harvest is contingent upon the *principle of giving* and the *pattern of receiving*. We can attack our lack by giving what we need or want to receive, because the harvest is guaranteed.

It is a sad commentary that so many of God's people never learn how to live like God wants them to live. When we come out of the world and into the kingdom of God, He wants us to adopt the Kingdom mindset. This is accomplished through God-given pastors and teachers who feed and instruct the people to live the way God wants them to live (Jer. 3:15).

The thief cometh not, but for to steal, and to kill, and to destroy: I am come that they might have life, and that they might have it more abundantly. (John 10:10)

Jesus came to display and distribute God's abundant living to humanity. Abundant living is reserved for the children of the Most High God, not the children of the devil. God has blessed His people with pastors in order to guarantee a good harvest in their lives. Therefore, God sends pastors to teach and prepare His people how to communicate; meaning to live according to what is being taught. Part of the pastor's purpose is to reveal how God wants us to live.

By now we understand the *purpose of our living* is to glorify God with our *time, talents, gifts, possessions,* and *money.* We are living because God has given us time and that's a blessing. He has also given us talents and that's a blessing. In 2nd Corinthians 10, the Apostle Paul says that no one should boast about their abilities because this would be considered comparing ourselves by ourselves (vs.12) and that is never wise.

If you are a skilled athlete, brilliant scientist, or gifted composer, that knowledge or talent is a gift from God. It is called *The blessing of the Lord or God's blessing.*

> *The blessing of the Lord, it maketh rich, and he addeth no sorrow with it. (Proverbs 10:22)*

God adds no sorrow with His blessing; it's a joyful experience. We don't serve a God of poverty but plenty. We serve a God that has more than enough. He has given us the ability to prosper and do well. Therefore, God wants us to use our blessings toward the advancement of His kingdom and this guarantees our harvest.

YOU WILL REAP WHATEVER YOU SOW

The principle of reaping and sowing brings us into God's harvest. Many believe this principle to only work in the area of money, but not so. Sowing and reaping works in any field. We can certainly reap God's harvest through right actions.

The Bible reveals a source of God's harvest called, *Shamgar's principle of deliverance.* In the Book of Judges, the 3rd Judge was a man by the name of Shamgar. Interestingly, one verse of Scripture unveils Shamgar's exploits with the enemies of Israel. Although much was not recorded about Shamgar, he was considered a judge like all his contemporaries who served God.

God used Shamgar to model what we need to learn. The first aspect Shamgar teaches is, *use what you have.* This lesson is simple because we cannot use what we do not have. Shamgar fought the Philistines by using what he had—an ox goad. Second, Shamgar *started where he was.* Where was he? Shamgar was on his farm and he never left it. Finally, this judge *did what he could.* What did Shamgar do? He killed six hundred Philistines with an ox goad. Shamgar was used by God to deliver Israel simply by: *"Using what he had, starting where he was and doing what he could."*

When you *use what you have, start where you are* and *do what you can,* God will do the super; you do the natural and this is what makes it supernatural. Through the supernatural you receive a good harvest. Jesus said, if we cannot be faithful in the least, we will not be faithful in much (Lu. 16:10). God starts us at the bottom and He moves us in such a way people around us recognize His favor. They will learn to see and say, *"It's all about Him and to God be the glory!"*

Beloved, don't look at your present circumstances and conclude, *"There's no hope."* You don't need a fortuitous event to occur when you have God's favor, all you need is a willing mind; just *"will"* to do it. Declare now, *"I will be who God has called me to be; my harvest is guaranteed!"*

Shamgar's Principle is a powerful standard of operation. It leaves no room for negotiation, debate or discussion. God will work out any situation for us if we are willing to *use what we have, start where we are and do what we can.*

God guarantees we are going to reap what we sow. All

of us are sowing something, and the harvest is guaranteed. Personally, I'm putting this concept of reaping and sowing in the framework of a positive mind-set. However, it must also be understood this principle works in the negative as well. We all know for every positive there's a corresponding negative. For instance, the opposite of light is dark and the opposite of abundance is poverty or lack.

> *Be not deceived; God is not mocked: for whatsoever a man soweth, that shall he also reap. (Galatians 6:7)*

Some people think they can play a game on God while they are really playing a game on themselves. Nothing is done behind closed doors; God sees everything. The Apostle Paul admonished us, *whatsoever a man sows that shall he also reap.* **The harvest is guaranteed!**

Understand when we sow, we will no doubt reap three things in our harvest.

1. *We reap what we sow.*
2. *We reap more than we sow.*
3. *We reap later than we have sown.*

Therefore, *if we are going to change the outcome of our living we have to change the income of our thinking.*

The congregation that I pastor consists of many giving and sowing people. As a church, we could not be where we are today if we had not sown or given what we have. The abundance of God is flowing in our ministry. When God brought us out of the world and into His kingdom, His treasures were open to us.

God wants His people to experience His abundant harvest. This is accomplished through the principle of sowing and reaping. This principle must become embedded in our hearts and minds. *As a man thinketh in his heart, so is he (Prov. 23:7).*

> For if there be first a willing mind, it is accepted according to that a man hath, and not according to that he hath not. (2 Corinthians 8:12)

God is looking for a willing mind. You must choose: are you going to be poor or live in the abundance of God? Even within a marriage, while living in the same house, sleeping in the same bed, one could be blessed while the other cursed.

I recall a long-time church member who was a giver and her husband was not a giver or member of any church. She was not working, but that did not hinder her from operating in the principle of sowing and reaping. Whenever she received a financial increase she faithful sowed into God's kingdom.

One day as they were walking to a local convenience store, her husband decided to teach her a lesson. He sarcastically remarked, *"You say God is the one supplying your needs? Well, I am the one that's working. I am the one taking care of you."*

The wife replied, *"No you're not taking care of me, God is taking care of me and He's providing for you."* The combative husband remarked, *"No, I'm taking care of you"* then he said, *"Well if God is the one that's taking care of you, let me see Him supply what you need!"*

By this time they were right in front of the store and the Holy Spirit spoke to the wife and said, *"Look down to your right."* She focused in that direction and there was some money lying on the ground. She walked over, picked it up and went in the store and purchased what she needed. Glory to God!

All God is asking for is a ready heart and mind concerning

sowing and reaping. He will put it in your hand if you have it in your heart and mind. **Your harvest is guaranteed!**

YOU'RE BLESSED FOR A GUARANTEED HARVEST

*And it shall come to pass, if thou shalt hearken
diligently unto the voice of the Lord thy God, to
observe and to do all his commandments which
I command thee this day, that the Lord thy God
will set thee on high above all nations of the
earth: And all these blessings shall come on thee,
and overtake thee... (Deuteronomy 28:1-2)*

The Lord has blessed you for a guaranteed harvest. Make no mistake about it, the blessings will come upon you and you cannot outrun them. The blessings will come and they will overtake you. They will get a hold of you so that you may have a hold on them.

*...If thou shalt hearken unto the voice of the Lord thy
God. Blessed shalt thou be in the city, and blessed
shalt thou be in the field. (Deuteronomy 28:2-3)*

Whether you are in North America, South America, Asia, Europe, Africa, etc., God is saying the blessings shall be in the city and in the field.

*Blessed shall be the fruit of thy body, and the fruit of
thy ground, and the fruit of thy cattle, the increase
of thy kine, and the flocks of thy sheep. Blessed shall
be thy basket and thy store. (Deuteronomy 28:4-5)*

When the Bible talks about a store in the above text, it's referring to bank accounts; checking and savings; IRA's and mutual funds. If you're currently without an account, open one as soon as possible. As you obey God's Word, watch and see Him increase your savings. Don't wait, step out by faith open your storehouse now!

God wants you to see His glory. He wants you to tell somebody about His goodness. He's looking to bless you coming in and going out; with an apartment or with a house. The Lord will bless, but you need to *start where you are, use what you have*, and *do what you can*.

> *Blessed shalt thou be when thou comest in, and*
> *blessed shalt thou be when thou goest out. The*
> *Lord shall cause thine enemies that rise up*
> *against thee to be smitten before thy face: they*
> *shall come out against thee one way, and flee*
> *before thee seven ways. (Deuteronomy 28:6-7)*

God said that He will cause your enemy to flee right in front of your face. In this case, the enemy is poverty.

> *The Lord shall command the blessing upon thee in thy*
> *storehouses, and in all that thou settest thine hand*
> *unto; and he shall bless thee in the land which the Lord*
> *thy God giveth thee. The Lord shall establish thee an*
> *holy people unto himself, as he hath sworn unto thee,*
> *if thou shalt keep the commandments of the Lord thy*
> *God, and walk in his ways. And all people of the earth*
> *shall see that thou art called by the name of the Lord;*
> *and they shall be afraid of thee. (Deuteronomy 28:8-10)*

The Lord has blessed you for a guaranteed harvest.

People in your neighborhood, on your job as well as your peers will have a reverence for you because you are called by the name of the Lord. There will be a reverence not to touch God's anointed and to do God's people no harm. The Lord's blessings will make you **too hot to handle**.

> *And the Lord shall make thee plenteous in goods, in the fruit of thy body, and in the fruit of thy cattle, and in the fruit of thy ground, in the land which the Lord swear unto thy fathers to give thee. The Lord shall open unto thee his good treasure, the heaven to give the rain unto thy land in his season, and to bless all the work of thine hand... (Deuteronomy 28:11-12)*

There is nothing more exciting than having the resources to give to others. You cannot give unless you have abundance. You cannot do what the Lord wants unless your cup is running over. Therefore, as you make up your mind to obey God in your giving; He will bless all the works of your hand.

I remember when God used my wife as a channel to encourage and bless me tremendously. I was looking for a job. The joy of the Lord was in my heart. It seemed like wherever I searched for employment opportunities, doors were being slammed shut.

On one occasion, I had just completed an interview. The man conducting the interview said to me, *"Well, we have other people on the list. If you are accepted, you'll hear from us within 24 hours."* I could sense they weren't interested in hiring me.

On my drive home, I stopped at a red light and the devil's presence entered my car. The enemy with sarcasm said, *"You let go of your previous life to serve God... what has God done for you? Now, you can't even find a job."* At the red light I broke down and cried. Then the Spirit of God repeated to me, *"Don't let go of your faith! Don't let go of your faith! Don't let go of your faith!"*

Upon hearing God's reassuring voice, I lifted up my eyes, wiped away the tears and began to sing. If the devil was still in the car he was forced to hear me sing God's praises all the way home.

Once I arrived home my wife Valerie asked, *"Did you get the job?"* Looking at my countenance she continued, *"I know you didn't."* Valerie further revealed that she had spoken with the president of the insurance company where she worked on my behalf. She explained my jobless situation and how I left my past to serve the Lord. After hearing my plight the president remarked, *"Tell your husband to come see me."*

The next morning I went to visit with the president of the company. I will admit I was quite apprehensive when I discovered about 50 people completing applications in the reception area. I approached the receptionist's desk and sheepishly announced, *"I'm here to see the president of the company."* When I gave my name I was amazed to hear the receptionist say, *"The president is waiting to see you."*

I entered the president's office and stated my name and she said, *"Your wife told me about your plight."* She got up from her desk, approached me with a warm friendly smile and said, *"I want you to know we have the same spiritual Father. You are hired!"*

Beloved, God is so good and He will open His treasures to you. No matter your situation; despair not. You are going to see the goodness of God in this season of your life. Don't turn back now, because He is turning the situation around. **Your harvest is guaranteed!**

CHAPTER 10
QUESTIONS FOR REFLECTION

According to the chapter, what does the
word communicate mean?

....

....

....

....

....

Write how you are using some of your time, talents,
gifts, possessions and money for God.

....

....

....

....

....

What are the three principles you
learned from Shamgar the judge?

....

....

....

....

....

What are the three results of every harvest?

....

....

....

....

....

How does God increase your savings?

....

....

....

....

....

....

....

....

....

....

....

11

HOW TO AVOID A BAD HARVEST

Be not deceived; God is not mocked: for whatsoever a man soweth, that shall he also reap. For he that soweth to his flesh shall of the flesh reap corruption; but he that soweth to the Spirit shall of the Spirit reap life everlasting. (Galatians 6:7-8)

GOD WANTS US TO KNOW how to avoid bad harvests. The way we avoid a bad harvest is by the grace of God and for the sake of Christ. Yes, it is for Christ's sake God cancels a bad harvest.

Bad things happen to all people and since we have sown negative and wrong things, the question becomes, "How do I avoid reaping the wrong I have sown?" 1 John 1:9 says to us that, *"If we confess our sins, he is faithful and just to forgive us our sins, and to cleanse us from all unrighteousness."*

WE MUST REPENT AND CONFESS

The way we get God to cancel a bad harvest is to repent and confess our sins. A bad harvest will not turn around until we turn around and turn to God. To repent means we cease from moving in our own direction; we change our minds concerning our decisions; we turn to God as our Director. Even as a pastor, dare I say, especially as a pastor, I need the Lord. Every day I have to lean on Jesus and turn to Him.

Jesus said:

> ...When you pray, say, Our Father which art in heaven, Hallowed be thy name. Thy kingdom come. Thy will be done, as in heaven, so in earth. Give us this day our daily bread. And forgive us our sins; for we also forgive every one that is indebted to us. And lead us not into temptation; but deliver us from evil. (Luke 11:2-4)

Every day, the same way you wash your face, you ought to wash your soul from anything that has contaminated it. Jesus washed the feet of his disciples because *"not all were clean"* (John 13:10-11). In like manner, we need to be washed every day by simply repenting and confessing our sins.

> If we confess our sins, he is faithful and just to forgive us our sins, and to cleanse us from all unrighteousness. If we say that we have not sinned, we make him a liar, and his word is not in us. (1 John 1:9-10)

Only God can clean up the mess that has been made in our lives. You may want to take an inventory of your soul. When was the last time you asked for the Lord's forgiveness? Some people go days, weeks, even months without asking for forgiveness. Then they are bewildered once they receive a bad harvest.

When Jesus announced to His disciples His departure, His encouragement was that He would send the Holy Spirit to comfort and correct.

And when he is come, he will reprove the world of sin,
and of righteousness, and of judgment: Of sin, because
they believe not on me; Of righteousness, because I
go to my Father, and ye see me no more; Of judgment,
because the prince of this world is judged. (John 16:8-11)

The Holy Spirit comes to:
1. *Reprove the world of sin*
2. *Promote righteousness*
3. *Pronounce judgment*

In a courtroom a judge will convict us of our **crime**; our conscience convicts us when we're **wrong**; only the Holy Spirit convicts us of our **sins**.

1st John 1:9 states, *"If we confess our sins..."* The word *confess* in this passage is the Greek word *homologeo*. This word carries the meaning *to say what God says*. When we counterfeit God's Word with our own, we are in essence holding Him in contempt. At this point, the Holy Spirit reveals our sin, and our response should be to confess it. If we fail to confess our revealed sin we end up reaping a bad harvest.

Fortunately, there is a way to avoid a bad harvest. If we repent, turn to God and say what He says, we can avoid a bad harvest. If God says something is a sin, we need to call it a sin. Failing to **confess it** causes us to **suppress it**, **depress it**, and eventually we will become **oppressed with it**.

GOD FORGIVES THE OFFENSE AND THE OFFENDER

By now, I hope you are fully persuaded that God will forgive you of your sins. However, maybe you need further assurance that He forgives the offender as well.

God will cancel out a bad harvest if we confess our sins.

And this is the confidence... if we ask any thing according to his will, he heareth us: And if we know that he hear us, whatsoever we ask, we know that we have the petitions that we desired of him. (1 John 5:14-15)

But to one who, not working [by the Law], trusts (believes fully) in Him Who justifies the ungodly, his faith is credited to him as righteousness (the standing acceptable to God). Thus David congratulates the man and pronounces a blessing on him to whom God credits righteousness apart from the works he does. (Romans 4:5-6 AMP)

David not only conveyed God forgives our sins, but the offender as well. Our offenses are no longer on God's records. When the devil tries to condemn us; God wants us to know, *"There is therefore now no condemnation to them which are in Christ Jesus, who walk not after the flesh, but after the Spirit"* (Romans 8:1). God will not condemn you because the bad harvest has been canceled.

Picture this; the devil will say to the Lord concerning our deeds, *"You remember what they did?"* God responds, *"I will not remember...it is gone."* The Lord throws our sin in the sea of forgetfulness (Micah 7:18-19) and there He places a sign that reads: *No fishing!* Now, He is not a God who forgets anything, He chooses to declare, *"I'll remember your sins and iniquities no more"* (Hebrews 8:12). Honestly, there are some things I do not want to reap. Many people cancel checks because of insufficient funds. Likewise, I want the Lord to cancel my bad harvest.

All of us, even after we received Jesus have sown some bad stuff. Even still, many people walk around as if nothing has happened. Remember, God is not mocked, we will reap what we sow. Therefore, when we plant bad seeds into the soil of our lives, we must seek God's forgiveness. The good news is *God forgives the sin and pardons the sinner.*

Make no mistake, we must repent and confess our sins immediately. We must never take the grace of God for granted or see His mercy as mediocre. God is faithful to forgive, but the problem is many people never ask for His forgiveness. To seek forgiveness takes humility.

David was a man after God's own heart, because he knew how to fall before God in humility. This very fact is evident in the 51st Psalm. God forgave David of his atrocities and He is still in the forgiving business. Forgiveness takes place when we *agree with the Holy Spirit about our sin, confess it* and *receive the forgiveness God bestows.*

There is a trilogy to sin that we must comprehend.

1. *Sin—**upward** against God; this is where it all starts.*

2. *Transgression—**outward** against others. To transgress is like transportation, we cut across a line that we should not cut across.*

3. *Iniquity—**inward** against ourselves. There is something bent and twisted on the inside of me.*

Once we understand the trilogy of sin we can identify and address it immediately. We address our sin by seeking God's grace and mercy. There is a revelation of a difference between grace and mercy.

- Grace is God's unmerited favor. God gives us what we don't deserve. *"For by grace are ye saved through faith; and that not of yourselves: it is the gift of God: Not of works, lest any man should boast"* (Ephesians 2:8-9).

- Mercy is God's forgiveness. God doesn't give us what we do deserve. *"It is of the Lord's mercies that we are not consumed, because his compassions fail not"* (Lamentations 3:22).

Choose today to have a fresh start with God. Don't claim a bad harvest. Allow God for Christ's sake to cancel a bad harvest and bring you into His blessings. The *pattern of receiving* is activated through the power of forgiveness. Move from being a sinner to a saint; from an offender to an overcomer by simply accepting the Father's forgiveness. Truly, He wants to forgive your sin and He possesses the power to pardon any offender.

Right now say the following prayer:

> *Father, I ask for your forgiveness and mercy. Like David, I ask you to search and try me. Whatever crooked way you find in me, make it straight. Lord I surrender this sin, transgression or iniquity to you now and I'm asking for Christ's sake; cancel a bad harvest in Jesus' name—Amen.*

GOD CANCELS BAD HARVESTS

God has the power to cancel bad harvests. We know God is the Creator because the Bible reveals this truth (Gen. 1:1). Psalm 24:1 reads, *"The earth is the Lord's, and the fullness thereof; the world, and they that dwell therein."* God owns it all. Therefore, He alone can cancel bad harvests.

Some mock God as if He is not there. God is the Creator but He is also the Redeemer and Owner. He paid the price with His blood to redeem us back. Therefore, all we have to do is ask to be forgiven and the bad harvest is canceled.

We have to belong to the family of God to have our bad harvest canceled. However, if you want to go to hell, the Lord will allow you to reap your bad harvest and go. If you want to go to heaven then ask God to cancel the bad seeds you have sown.

> *He that observes the wind shall not*
> *sow... (Ecclesiastes 11:4)*

The *pattern of receiving* deals with the good seed we must sow. Some people always have an excuse why they cannot or will not give. These are people that observe the wind (have an excuse). Everyone sows something during their life span. We sow our time, talents, gifts, possessions, and money. However, we must choose to sow to our flesh or sow because of the Holy Spirit's conviction to obey Jesus. When we obey God it opens the *pattern of receiving* and God meets our needs.

> *For they have sown the wind, and they shall*
> *reap the whirlwind... (Hosea 8:7)*

Remember the principle concerning sowing:

> *1. We reap what we sow.*
> *2. We reap more than we sow.*
> *3. We reap later than we have sown.*

> *Come, and let us return unto the LORD: for he hath*
> *torn, and he will heal us; he hath smitten, and he will*
> *bind us up. After two days will he revive us: in the*
> *third day he will raise us up, and we shall live in his*

sight. Then shall we know, if we follow on to know the
LORD: his going forth is prepared as the morning;
and he shall come unto us as the rain, as the latter
and former rain unto the earth. (Hosea 6:1-3)

The same way God cancelled a bad harvest for Israel in Hosea's time, He will cancel a bad harvest for you today. Your harvest will be plentiful; it will be a good harvest not a bad one.

The devil is bringing a whirlwind. However, throughout the Bible, God canceled bad harvests. Bad things happen to all people. As long as you are in this world the rains will descend, the floods will come and the winds will blow (Matthew 7:25). It's true, *we reap what we sow*; *more than what we sow*; and *later than when we have sown it*. However, there are some things we do not want to reap.

God was bringing judgment to the Ninevites because of their sins, transgressions and their iniquities. Therefore, God told Jonah to go and preach to Nineveh, but Jonah caught a ship going to Tarshish. Jonah was going in the other direction. In essence, Jonah was sowing disobedience and because of this, he paid his on fair (Jonah 1:3).

But the LORD sent out a great wind into the sea,
and there was a mighty tempest in the sea, so that
the ship was like to be broken. Then the mariners
were afraid, and cried every man unto his god,
and cast forth the wares that were in the ship into
the sea, to lighten it of them. But Jonah was gone
down into the sides of the ship; and he lay, and
was fast asleep. So the shipmaster came to him,
and said unto him, What meanest thou, O sleeper?

arise, call upon thy God, if so be that God will
think upon us, that we perish not." (Jonah 1:4-6)

Everyone was crying to their gods in the midst of the storm except Jonah. He was asleep! The mariners brought Jonah up and said why aren't you praying? Jonah replied because my God is the God of the heavens and of the seas, He is God and God alone.

After spending 3 days in the belly of a great fish Jonah realized the Lord was not only the God of the heavens, but also of the harvest. Therefore, Jonah prayed:

I went down to the bottoms of the mountains; the
earth with her bars was about me forever. Yet hast
thou brought up my life from corruption, O LORD
my God. When my soul fainted within me, I remem-
bered the LORD: and my prayer came in unto thee,
into thine holy temple. They that observe lying
vanities forsake their own mercy. (Jonah 2:6-8)

While in the belly of the fish praising God, Jonah said:

...I will pay that that I have vowed. Salvation is of
the LORD. And the LORD spake unto the fish, and it
vomited out Jonah upon the dry land. (Jonah 2:9-10)

When Jonah prayed, the Lord commanded the fish to spew him out. When Jonah came out of that fish's belly he discovered that he was at Nineveh; the place that God had commanded him to go. In Nineveh Jonah became a sign of God's mercy and that God can cancel a bad harvest!

But let man and beast be covered with sackcloth,
and cry mightily unto God: yea, let them turn

*every one from his evil way, and from the vio-
lence that is in their hands. Who can tell if God
will turn and repent, and turn away from his
fierce anger, that we perish not? (Jonah 3:8-9)*

The people of Nineveh responded by saying, *"Who can
tell? Perhaps God will be merciful to us and turn away from
his fierce anger that we perish not."* God saw their works that
they turned from their evil way; and God repented. Now if
God can repent, shouldn't we?

Beloved, God is merciful. It is His desire to cancel a bad
harvest so let Him do it by confessing your sins and receiving
His forgiveness. You reap what you sow. Therefore, begin
sowing for a good harvest and enjoy the life God has designed
for you.

CHAPTER ELEVEN
QUESTIONS FOR REFLECTION

Do you need God to cancel a bad harvest? If so, you must repent and confess to Him. Write the harvest you need canceled.

....

....

....

....

....

....

What does it mean to repent?

....

....

....

....

How do you avoid a bad harvest?

....

....

....

....

Name and explain the trilogy to sin you must comprehend.

....

....

....

....

....

....

Name the principle of sowing:

....

....

....

....

....

....

....

....

Name and explain a good harvest you need. What
should you do to receive it from God?

....

....

....

....

....

....

....

....

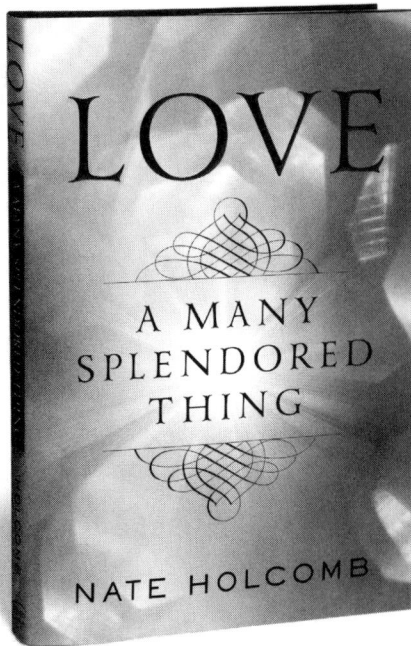